Understanding

The Law Firm of F.

As a firm, we have represented victims ~~of~~ ~~commercial~~ vehicle collisions involving serious personal injury or wrongful ~~death in more~~ than 20 different states across the country and have handled over 150 commercial vehicle cases where the verdict or settlement was greater than $1 million dollars. To learn more about out firm, please visit our website at *www.thetruckingattorneys.com.*

We have taken our extensive experience and knowledge of truck accident law and created *Understanding Motor Carrier Claims*, Sixth Edition. Our main goal in publishing this guide is to provide an in-depth analysis of the complexities of motor carrier law so other practitioners can understand the basics of trucking claims. The biggest mistake a lawyer can make is treating a trucking case like a typical automobile accident. We hope our guide will provide the reader with insight into the multitude of issues presented by a commercial vehicle case. We have also created a password-protected online portal containing all our depositions and forms for trucking cases located at *www.frg-law.com/portal.*

If you have any questions about trucking law, please do not hesitate to call us or send us an e-mail.

Joseph A. Fried

Brian D. "Buck" Rogers

Michael L. Goldberg

Fried Rogers Goldberg LLC
Atlanta, Georgia

Tel: 404.591.1800
     877.591.1801

Email: joe@frg-law.com   Cell: 404.429.6677
       buck@frg-law.com   404.216.5978
       michael@frg-law.com   404.840.2084

Table of Contents

I.	Information on Motor Carriers	5
II.	Theories of Liability	18
III.	Driver Qualifications	38
IV.	The Commercial Driver's License Manual	47
V.	Alcohol and Controlled Substance Testing	55
VI.	Hours of Service Regulations	66
VII.	Federal Motor Carrier Safety Regulations	70
VIII.	Electronic Control Module (ECM)	90
IX.	Computer Data & Systems	97
X.	Insurance Coverage	109
XI.	Types of Trucking Cases	115
XII.	Handling a Trucking Case	119
XIII.	Other Types of Accidents Related to Commercial Vehicles	121
XIV.	Principles of Accident Reconstruction in Commercial Vehicle Cases	127
XV.	Cellphone Evidence	135
XVI.	Deposing the Truck Driver & Safety Director	137
XVII.	Trucking Checklists	140
XVIII.	Appendix of Forms	146
XIX.	Index	151

I. Information on Motor Carriers

A. Basics of Interstate Versus Intrastate Motor Carriers

There are two kinds of motor carriers: (1) interstate carriers and (2) intrastate carriers. An interstate carrier provides transportation services across state borders and is required to register with the Secretary of Transportation[1] while an intrastate carrier has its operations entirely within one state and does not affect interstate commerce.[2] Because the federal government is limited to regulating only "interstate commerce," federal regulations governing motor carriers are only applicable to interstate carriers, and intrastate carriers only have to comply with state laws governing commercial motor vehicles.[3] Many states, through their legislature or Public Service Commission, have adopted the federal regulations governing motor carriers as applicable to intrastate carriers and as a practical matter, removed the distinction between the two kinds of carriers.[4] The importance of federal regulations on the motor carrier industry is discussed throughout this handbook, and it is critical to an analysis of a trucking claim to determine the applicability of these regulations to the carrier's operations.

Practice Pointer: If a motor carrier operates as an intrastate carrier, review state laws to determine the applicability of federal regulations to the carrier's operations.

B. Federal Registration

Before a motor carrier can begin interstate operations, the carrier must register with the Federal Motor Carrier Safety Administration ("FMCSA"), obtain a USDOT number, and obtain operating authority from the FMCSA.[5] The motor carrier must mark each commercial motor vehicle with the name of the motor carrier and the USDOT number.[6] The process of registering with the FMCSA through the Unified Registration System (URS) system and online OP-1 form[7] is shown below:

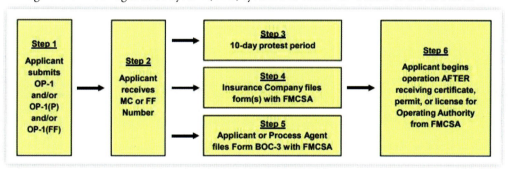

The motor carrier must register on-line through the URS in order to obtain authority.

---

[1] 49 U.S.C. § 13901.
[2] Progressive Casualty Insurance Co. v. Hoover, 809 A.2d 353 (Pa. 2002).
[3] Texas v. United States, 866 F.2d 1546 (5th Cir. 1989).
[4] See Transportation Rules of the Georgia Public Service Commission.
[5] 49 C.F.R. § 385.301.
[6] 49 C.F.R. § 390.21.
[7] 49 C.F.R. § 365.105B.

The online OP-1 form also has a safety certification section and an oath that must be taken by the motor carrier's owner or designated agent.

Form OP-1 (Revised: 09/27/2013)

SECTION IV — Safety Certification *(for vehicle-operating applicants only).* Select only one.

30. APPLICANTS SUBJECT TO FEDERAL MOTOR CARRIER SAFETY REGULATIONS.
If you will operate vehicles of more than 10,000 pounds GVWR and are, thus, subject to pertinent portions of the USDOT's Federal Motor Carrier Safety Regulations (FMCSRs) at 49 CFR, Chapter 3, Subchapter B (Parts 350-399), you must certify as follows:

Applicant has access to and is familiar with all applicable USDOT regulations relating to the safe operation of commercial vehicles and the safe transportation of hazardous materials, and will comply with these regulations. In so certifying, applicant is verifying that, at a minimum, it: (1) Has in place a system and an individual responsible for ensuring overall compliance with FMCSRs. (2) Can produce a copy of the FMCSRs and the Hazardous Materials Transportation Regulations. (3) Has in place a driver safety training/orientation program. (4) Has prepared and maintains an accident register (49 CFR 390.15). (5) Is familiar with DOT regulations governing driver qualifications and has in place a system for overseeing driver qualification requirements (49 CFR 391). (6) Has in place policies and procedures consistent with USDOT regulations governing driving and operational safety of motor vehicles, including drivers' hours of service and vehicle inspection, repair, and maintenance (49 CFR 392, 395, and 396). (7) Is familiar with, and will have in place on the appropriate effective date, a system for complying with USDOT regulations governing alcohol and controlled substances testing requirements (49 CFR 382 and 40). ○ Yes

The OP-1 form requires a compliance certification that the motor carrier will follow the safety regulations.

SECTION VIII

Applicant's Oath

This oath applies to all supplemental filings to this application. <u>The signature must be that of applicant, not legal representative.</u>

I, _____, verify under penalty of
   Name and title

perjury, under the laws of the United States of America, that all information supplied on this form or relating to this application is true and correct. Further, I certify that I am qualified and authorized to file this application. I know that willful misstatements or omissions of material facts constitute Federal criminal violations punishable under 18 U.S.C. 1001 by imprisonment up to 5 years and fines up to $10,000 for each offense. Additionally, these misstatements are punishable as perjury under 18 U.S.C. 1621, which provides for fines up to $2,000 or imprisonment up to 5 years for each offense.

I further certify under penalty of perjury, under the laws of the United States, that I have not been convicted, after September 1, 1989, of any Federal or State offense involving the distribution or possession of a controlled substance, or that if I have been so convicted, I am not ineligible to receive Federal benefits, either by court order or operation of law, pursuant to Section 5301 of the Anti-Drug Abuse Act of 1988 (21 U.S.C. 862).

Signature _____ Date _____

On the OP-1 form, the applicant must certify that he is familiar with the FMCSR."

A person may obtain a copy of the application for a motor carrier through the FMCSA.[8]

Under the Uniform Carrier Registration System (UCRS), the motor carrier designates as its "Base State" the State where it maintains its principal place of business.[9] The motor carrier registers with the UCRS through its Base State and must pay a standard fee to the UCRS as set out by the UCR agreement rather than being subject to the fees and registration outlined by individual states.[10] If the motor carrier is registered as an interstate carrier, a State cannot require the motor carrier to obtain intrastate authority or require the motor carrier to make any insurance filings.[11]

As part of the federal registration scheme, each motor carrier must designate a registered agent for service of process in each state that the carrier operates.[12] A registered agent may be canceled only by designating a substitute agent.[13] A form for the designation of a registered agent must be filed with the FMCSA.[14]

---

[8] 49 C.F.R. § 365.117.
[9] 49 U.S.C. § 14504a(a)(2).
[10] 49 U.S.C. § 14504a(f).
[11] 49 U.S.C. § 14504a(c)(1)(D).
[12] 49 C.F.R. § 366.3 & 366.4(a).
[13] 49 C.F.R. § 366.6.
[14] 49 C.F.R. § 366.2.

In 2004, a safety permit program was instituted for the registration of all carriers of hazardous materials.[15] The safety permit program applies to both intrastate and interstate carriers.[16] The FMCSA will not issue a safety permit to any carrier that is in the top 30% of the national crash average as indicated in the Motor Carrier Management Information System (MCMIS).[17] As required by the program, intrastate carriers of hazardous materials must apply for a USDOT number and be subject to a compliance review but are not subject to additional federal safety regulations.[18] Intrastate carriers of hazardous materials, like interstate carriers, must also file a motor carrier identification report and mark their vehicles with the motor carrier's name and USDOT number.[19]

**Practice Pointer: The application forms can be used to show that the motor carrier violated its oath to understand and follow federal regulations.

C. Safety Fitness Ratings

An interstate carrier is required to meet minimum safety fitness standards.[20] In order to meet these standards, a carrier must have adequate safety management controls in place to reduce the risks associated with (1) commercial driver's license standard violations, (2) inadequate levels of financial responsibility, (3) the use of unqualified drivers, (4) improper use and driving of motor vehicles, (5) unsafe vehicles operating on the highways, (6) failure to maintain accident registers and copies of accident reports, (7) the use of fatigued drivers, (8) inadequate inspection, repair and maintenance of vehicles, (9) improper transportation of hazardous materials, and (10) motor vehicle accidents and hazardous materials incidents.[21] The Federal Highway Administration ("FHWA") performs an annual compliance review on each carrier and assigns it a safety rating.[22] A carrier's safety rating is based on the adequacy of safety management controls, frequency and severity of regulatory violations, frequency and severity of regulatory violations identified in roadside inspections, the number and frequency of out-of-service driver/vehicle violations, frequency of accidents, and the number and severity of violations of state safety rules.[23]

The FMCSA provides notice to the carrier of its safety rating and reports a list of compliance deficiencies which the motor carrier must correct.[24] A "satisfactory" rating means that the motor carrier has in place adequate safety management controls to meet the safety fitness standards.[25] A "conditional" or "unsatisfactory" rating means a motor carrier does not have adequate safety management controls in place.[26] A carrier rated "unsatisfactory" is prohibited from operating commercial vehicles.[27] A carrier may petition the FMCSA for a review of its rating after taking corrective actions to remedy any problems and defects in its operations.[28] Motor carriers domiciled in Mexico are subject to intensified monitoring by frequent safety audits and inspections.[29]

---

[15] 49 C.F.R. § 385.401.
[16] 49 C.F.R. § 385.403.
[17] 49 C.F.R. § 385.407.
[18] 49 C.F.R. § 385.403.
[19] 49 C.F.R. § 390.3.
[20] 49 C.F.R. § 385.1.
[21] 49 C.F.R. § 385.5.
[22] 49 C.F.R. § 385.9.
[23] 49 C.F.R. § 385.7.
[24] 49 C.F.R. § 385.11.
[25] 49 C.F.R. § 385.3.
[26] 49 C.F.R. § 385.3.
[27] 49 C.F.R. § 385.13(a).
[28] 49 C.F.R. § 385.17.
[29] 49 C.F.R. § 385.103.

D. Safety and Fitness Electronic Records (SAFER)

The Safety and Fitness Electronic Records (SAFER) System was designed by the Federal Motor Carrier Safety Administration (FMCSA) to provide the public and trucking industry service providers with information on motor carriers. To access information on a motor carrier, first proceed to www.safer.fmcsa.dot.gov. Under the heading FMCSA searches, click on the section "Company Snapshot." After clicking on this section, a search can be conducted on a motor carrier based on the motor carrier's name, US DOT Number or MC/MX Number.

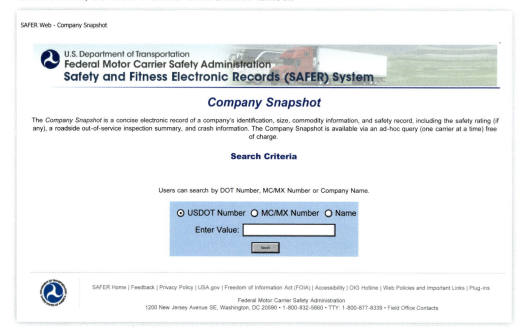

Enter the appropriate information on the motor carrier to pull up the company snapshot. The Company Snapshot includes background information on the motor carrier as well as general information on inspections, crashes and the carrier's safety rating. We have included the company snapshot on Federal Express Corporation:

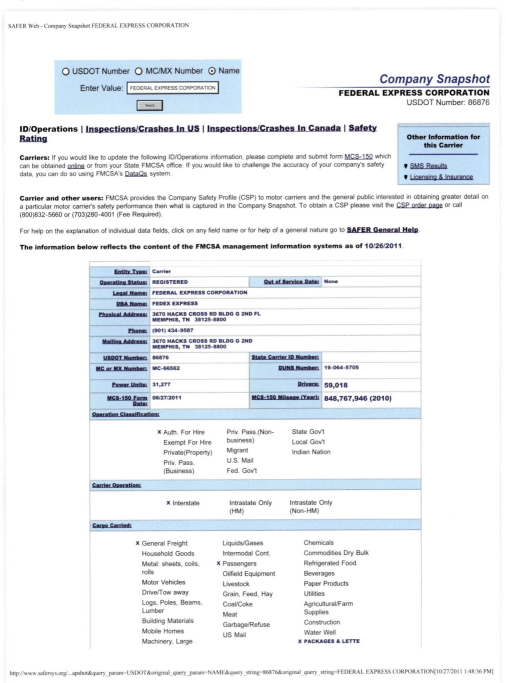

This screen shows the background information on the motor carrier.

ID/Operations | Inspections/Crashes In US | Inspections/Crashes In Canada | Safety Rating

US Inspection results for 24 months prior to: 10/26/2011

Total inspections: 3168

Note: Total inspections may be less than the sum of vehicle, driver, and hazmat inspections. Go to Inspections Help for further information.

Inspections:

Inspection Type	Vehicle	Driver	Hazmat
Inspections	2424	2810	193
Out of Service	156	21	12
Out of Service %	6.4%	0.7%	6.2%
Nat'l Average % (2009- 2010)	20.72%	5.51%	4.50%

Crashes reported to FMCSA by states for 24 months prior to: 10/26/2011

Crashes:

Type	Fatal	Injury	Tow	Total
Crashes	7	208	299	514

ID/Operations | Inspections/Crashes In US | Inspections/Crashes In Canada | Safety Rating

Canadian Inspection results for 24 months prior to: 10/26/2011

Total inspections: 0

Note: Total inspections may be less than the sum of vehicle and driver inspections. Go to Inspections Help for further information.

Inspections:

Inspection Type	Vehicle	Driver
Inspections	0	0
Out of Service	0	0
Out of Service %	0%	0%

Crashes results for 24 months prior to: 10/26/2011

Crashes:

Type	Fatal	Injury	Tow	Total
Crashes	0	0	0	0

This screen shows the inspection summary and crash information.

Rating Date:	05/26/1994	Review Date:	03/12/2004
Rating:	Satisfactory	Type:	

SAFER Home | Feedback | Privacy Policy | USA.gov | Freedom of Information Act (FOIA) | Accessibility | OIG Hotline | Web Policies and Important Links | Plug-ins

Federal Motor Carrier Safety Administration
1200 New Jersey Avenue SE, Washington, DC 20590 • 1-800-832-5660 • TTY: 1-800-877-8339 • Field Office Contacts

This screen shows the safety rating for the trucking company.

In the upper right hand corner of the Company Snapshot screen, you can click on "Licensing and Insurance" to learn about the carrier's insurance background.

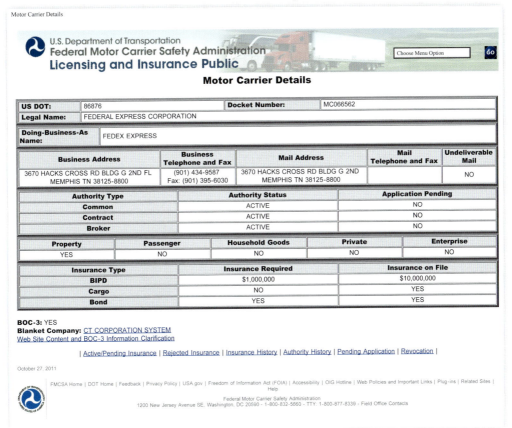

If you click on "Insurance History" at the bottom of the screen in the section under Licensing and Insurance, you will be provided with the name of insurers for the motor carrier for the last several years.

Insurance History

Insurance History

US DOT:	86876	Docket Number:	MC066562
Legal Name:	FEDERAL EXPRESS CORPORATION		

Form	Type	Insurance Carrier	Policy/Surety	Coverage From	Coverage To	Effective Date From	Effective Date To
91X	BIPD/Primary	ACE AMERICAN INSURANCE COMPANY	ISA H08630860	$0	$10,000,000	10/01/2010	10/01/2011 Replaced
91X	BIPD/Primary	ACE AMERICAN INSURANCE COMPANY	ISA H08581034	$0	$10,000,000	10/01/2009	10/01/2010 Replaced
91X	BIPD/Primary	ACE AMERICAN INSURANCE COMPANY	ISA H08242604	$0	$10,000,000	10/01/2008	10/01/2009 Replaced
91X	BIPD/Primary	ACE AMERICAN INSURANCE COMPANY	ISA H08215844	$0	$10,000,000	10/01/2007	10/01/2008 Replaced
91X	BIPD/Primary	ACE AMERICAN INSURANCE COMPANY	ISA H0822500A	$0	$10,000,000	10/01/2006	10/01/2007 Replaced
91X	BIPD/Primary	FACTORY MUTUAL INSURANCE COMPANY	JB194	$0	$5,000,000	10/04/2003	10/04/2003 Replaced
91X	BIPD/Primary	FACTORY MUTUAL INSURANCE COMPANY	JB194	$0	$5,000,000	10/04/2003	10/04/2003 Replaced
91X	BIPD/Primary	FACTORY MUTUAL INSURANCE COMPANY	JB194	$0	$5,000,000	10/04/2003	09/25/2006 Cancelled
91X	BIPD/Primary	ACE AMERICAN INSURANCE COMPANY	ISA H 079 341 05	$0	$10,000,000	10/01/2003	10/04/2003 Replaced
91X	BIPD/Primary	SENTRY INSURANCE A MUTUAL COMPANY	900165202	$0	$1,000,000	08/16/2000	08/16/2000 Replaced
91X	BIPD/Primary	SENTRY INSURANCE A MUTUAL COMPANY	900165202	$0	$5,000,000	08/16/2000	10/01/2003 Cancelled
91X	BIPD/Primary	SENTRY INSURANCE A MUTUAL COMPANY	90-01652-02	$0	$5,000,000	08/16/1998	02/16/2001 Name Changed
91X	BIPD/Primary	SENTRY INSURANCE A MUTUAL COMPANY	90-01652-02	$0	$5,000,000	08/16/1990	08/16/1998 Replaced
34	CARGO	FACTORY MUTUAL INSURANCE COMPANY	JB194	$0	$5,000*	10/04/2003	10/01/2003 Replaced
34	CARGO	FACTORY MUTUAL INSURANCE COMPANY	JB194	$0	$5,000*	10/01/2003	10/01/2003 Replaced
34	CARGO	SENTRY INSURANCE A MUTUAL COMPANY	90-01652-05	$0	$5,000*	08/16/2000	10/01/2003 Cancelled
34	CARGO	SENTRY INSURANCE A MUTUAL COMPANY	900165202	$0	$5,000*	08/16/1988	02/16/2001 Name Changed
84	SURETY	TRAVELERS CASUALTY & SURETY CO. OF AMERICA	104536311	$0	$10,000*	06/07/2005	06/07/2005 Replaced
84	SURETY	NATIONAL FIRE INSURANCE CO. OF HARTFORD	123938433	$0	$10,000*	01/05/2005	06/07/2005 Replaced
84	SURETY	NATIONAL FIRE INS. CO. OF HARTFORD	123938433	$0	$10,000*	01/05/2001	01/05/2005 Replaced
84	SURETY	NATIONAL FIRE INSURANCE CO. OF HARTFORD	123938433	$0	$10,000*	06/07/1993	02/16/2001 Name Changed
84	SURETY	NATIONAL FIRE INSURANCE CO. OF HARTFORD	123938433	$0	$10,000*	06/07/1993	01/05/2001 Replaced

* If a carrier is in compliance, the amount of coverage will always be shown as the required Federal minimum ($5,000 per vehicle, $10,000 per occurrence for cargo insurance and $10,000 for bond/trust fund). The carrier may actually have higher levels of coverage.

| Carrier Details | Active/Pending Insurance | Rejected Insurance | Authority History | Pending Application | Revocation |

October 27, 2011

FMCSA Home | DOT Home | Feedback | Privacy Policy | USA.gov | Freedom of Information Act (FOIA) | Accessibility | OIG Hotline | Web Policies and Important Links | Plug-ins | Related Sites | Help

http://li-public.fmcsa.dot.gov/...pcant_id=3258&pv_legal_name=FEDERAL^EXPRESS^CORPORATION&pv_pref_docket=MC066562&pv_usdot_no=86876&pv_vpath=LIVIEW[10/27/2011 1:53:51 PM]

If you click on the entity identified next to "Blanket Company" at the bottom left hand side of the screen in the section under Licensing and Insurance, you will be provided with the agents for service of process for the motor carrier in all the states that the carrier has operations.

Process Agents for: CT CORPORATION SYSTEM

U.S. Department of Transportation
Federal Motor Carrier Safety Administration
Licensing and Insurance Public

Process Agents for: CT CORPORATION SYSTEM

State	Representative Name/ Company Name	Address
AK	C T CORPORTATION SYSTEM	801 WEST TENTH STREET, SUITE 300 JUNEAU AK, 99801
AL	THE CORPORATION COMPANY	2 NORTH JACKSON STREET, SUITE 605 MONTGOMERY AL, 36104
AR	THE CORPORATION COMPANY	425 WEST CAPITOL AVE, SUITE 1700 LITTLE ROCK AR, 72201
AZ	C T CORPORATION SYSTEM	3225 N. CENTRAL AVENUE PHOENIX AZ, 85012
CA	C T CORPORATION SYSTEM	818 WEST SEVENTH STREET LOS ANGELES CA, 90017
CO	THE CORPORATION COMPANY	1675 BROADWAY, SUITE 1200 DENVER CO, 80202
CT	C T CORPORATION SYSTEM	ONE COMMERCIAL PLAZA HARTFORD CT, 06103
DC	C T CORPORATION SYSTEM	1015 15TH STREET, NW, SUITE 1000 WASHINGTON DC, 20005
DE	THE CORPORATION TRUST COMPANY	1209 ORANGE STREET WILMINGTON DE, 19801
FL	C T CORPORATION SYSTEM	1200 SOUTH PINE ISLAND ROAD PLANTATION FL, 33324
GA	C T CORPORATION SYSTEM	1201 PEACHTREE STREET, N.E. ATLANTA GA, 30361
HI	THE CORPORATION COMPANY, INC.	1000 BISHOP STREET HONOLULU HI, 96813
IA	C T CORPORATION SYSTEM	2222 GRAND AVENUE DES MOINES IA, 50312
ID	C T CORPORATION SYSTEM	300 NORTH 6TH STREET BOISE ID, 83702
IL	C T CORPORATION SYSTEM	208 LA SALLE STREET CHICAGO IL, 60604
IN	C T CORPORATION SYSTEM	251 E. OHIO STREET, SUITE 1100 INDIANAPOLIS IN, 46204
KS	THE CORPORATION COMPANY, INC.	112 SW 7TH STREET, SUITE 3C TOPEKA KS, 66603
KY	C T CORPORATION SYSTEM	KENTUCKY HOME LIFE BLDG. LOUISVILLE KY, 40202
LA	C T CORPORATION SYSTEM	8550 UNITED PLAZA BOULEVARD BATON ROUGE LA, 70809
MA	C T CORPORATION SYSTEM	101 FEDERAL STREET BOSTON MA, 02110
MD	THE CORPORATION TRUST INCORPORATED	300 EAST LOMBARD STREET BALTIMORE MD, 21202
ME	C T CORPORATION SYSTEM	ONE PORTLAND SQUARE PORTLAND ME, 04101
MI	THE CORPORATION COMPANY	30600 TELEGRAPH ROAD BINGHAM FARMS MI, 48025
MN	C T CORPORATION SYSTEM, INC.	401 SECOND AVENUE SOUTH MINNEAPOLIS MN, 55401
MO	C T CORPORATION SYSTEM	120 SOUTH CENTRAL AVENUE CLAYTON MO, 63105
MS	C T CORPORATION	645 LAKELAND EAST DR, SUITE 101 FLOWOOD MS, 39232
MT	C T CORPORATION SYSTEM	40 WEST LAWRENCE, SUITE A HELENA MT, 59624
NC	C T CORPORATION	225 HILLSBOROUGH STREET

http://li-public.fmcsa.dot.gov/LIVIEW/pkg_html.prc_proc_servers?cov_id=7&pv_vpath=LIVIEW&pv_web_user_type=P[10/27/2011 1:55:27 PM]

This screen shows registered agents for service of process on the motor carrier.

If you return to the Company Snapshot screen and click on "SMS Results" in the top right hand side of the screen, you will be provided with additional information from the Safety Management System (SMS) concerning the safety scores of the motor carrier.

**Practice Pointer: Lookup information on the trucking company, its insurance history and its safety record at www.safer.fmcsa.dot.gov.

E.   Safety Management System (SMS)

In December of 2010, the FMCSA rolled out the Compliance, Safety & Accountability (CSA) System. As part of CSA, the FMCSA designed the Safety Management System (SMS) to collect data from truck drivers and motor carriers in order to assess the overall safety of the motor carrier. SMS focuses on seven Behavior Analysis and Safety Improvement Categories (BASIC). These categories include (1) Unsafe Driving- operating a commercial vehicle by drivers in a careless or dangerous manner; (2) Fatigued Driving – operating a commercial vehicle while ill, fatigued or in non-compliance with hours of service regulations; (3) Driver Fitness – operation of commercial vehicle by drivers who are unfit due to lack of training, experience or medical qualifications; (4) Controlled Substances/Alcohol – operation of commercial vehicle by impaired drivers; (5) Vehicle Maintenance – failure to properly maintain a vehicle; (6) Cargo-Related – failure to properly load a vehicle, dropped or spilled cargo, overloading and unsafe hazardous material handling; and (7) Crash indicator – history of high crash involvement based on frequency and severity of crashes. The SMS System collects this data over a 24 month period, and some of this information is available to the public. Although information is collected on individual drivers, the public cannot access information on an individual driver and only has limited access to information on the motor carrier. The SMS System identifies the scores of the motor carrier in that category and how high the score must go to warrant intervention.

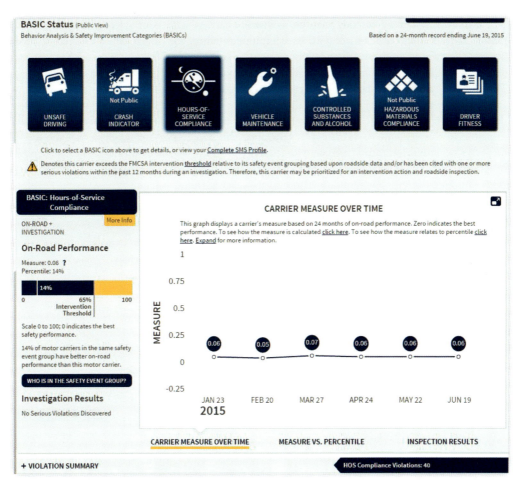

You can click on any icon, such as Hours of Service, and obtain the report for that BASIC category and see how close the motor carrier's score is to the threshold for intervention.

The SMS System allows the FMCSA to identify carriers with poor safety performance. If a motor carrier has any deficiencies with its safety performance, the carrier will be subject to CSA intervention ranging from a warning letter to an out-of-service order. The motor carrier has access to its SMS results and is encouraged by the FMCSA to dispute the validity of any reported information. The SMS and related CSA intervention results can establish a pattern of poor safety and a failure to address problems with safety in a timely manner. However, the website specifically states: "Readers should not draw conclusions about a carrier's overall safety condition simply based on the data displayed in this system." As such, expert testimony will be necessary to establish that the motor carrier's SMS results indicate a problem with its safety program. You can view the entire SMS Profile by clicking on the link for "Complete SMS Profile" on the left side of the screen.

You can also download a complete list of all inspections and results that went into the SMS data by clicking on "Download" on the left hand side of the screen.

Practice Pointer: Download data from the SMS System on all inspections and citations given to a trucking company in the last 24 months.

II. Theories of Liability

A. Employer Liability

When the driver is an actual employee of the trucking company, sometimes referred to as a "company driver," the company's liability is governed by state common law theories of agency.[30] In such a situation, the motor carrier, as the employer of the driver, is only responsible for the driver's actions while he is acting within the scope of his employment.[31] A driver acts within the scope of his employment if his actions further the carrier's business in any manner even if the driver's conduct also benefits himself.[32] A driver who violates a trucking company's policies or procedures still acts within the scope of his employment while his activities are related to the company's business.[33] Similarly, a driver's use of alcohol or illegal drugs does not take him out of the scope of his employment when driving a commercial vehicle.[34] When a driver who has just delivered a load is operating a tractor-trailer while waiting for another dispatch, a jury issue exists as to whether he is acting within the scope of his employment with the motor carrier since his actions are not purely personal.[35]

A driver is outside the scope of his employment as a matter of law when he drops off his trailer at a carrier's facility and then departs on a personal mission.[36] A carrier cannot be held vicariously liable for the rape of a hitchhiker by a long haul driver since his actions are not in furtherance of the interests of his employer and are clearly outside the scope of his employment.[37] However, most jurisdictions hold that common carriers of passengers are responsible for assaults and intentional torts against passengers by an employee, even if the employee's motivation was entirely personal, under the theory that a passenger carrier has a non-delegable duty to protect its passengers.[38]

Practice Pointer: If the driver is employed by the trucking company, review state law governing agency.

B. Lease Liability

Federal regulations require a trucking company that leases a vehicle and driver, commonly referred to as an "owner/operator" lease, to have "exclusive possession, control and use" of the leased vehicle.[39] Courts have used this requirement to hold the trucking company responsible for accidents caused by a leased driver's negligence under the theory that the company, by allowing a driver to operate a commercial vehicle under its interstate authorization, permits an otherwise unregulated truck and driver to be on the road in interstate commerce.[40] Prior to the 1986 amendment to the Federal Motor Carrier Safety Regulations ("FMCSR"), a lessee motor carrier was required to remove its placards and other identification markers from its vehicle before returning the equipment to the owner and terminating the lease.[41] Based on this former regulation, courts created the doctrine of "logo" or "placard" liability by focusing on the use of a motor carrier's placards as a method of imputing liability to the carrier.[42] A motor carrier could not eliminate its responsibility for the operation of leased equipment until it removed the identifying placards from the unit even if it had

---

[30] Warner Trucking, Inc. v. Carolina Casualty Insurance Co., 686 N.E.2d 102 (Ind. 1997).
[31] Id. at 105.
[32] Id.
[33] Id. at 106.
[34] Frederick v. Swift Transportation Co., 616 F.3d 1074 (10th Cir. 2010).
[35] Wright v. Transus, Inc., 434 S.E.2d 786 (Ga. 1993).
[36] Parker v. Erixon, 473 S.E.2d 421 (N.C. 1996).
[37] C.C. v. Roadrunner Trucking, Inc., 823 F.Supp. 913 (D.Utah 1993).
[38] Rabon v. Guardsmark, Inc., 571 F.2d 1277 (4th Cir. 1978); Commodore Cruise Line, Ltd. v. Kormendi, 344 So.2d 896 (Fla. 1977); St. Michelle v. Catania, 250 A.2d 874 (Md. 1969); Berger v. Southern Pacific Co., 300 P.2d 170 (Cal. 1956); But see Sebastian v. District of Columbia, 636 A.2d 958 (D.C. 1994).
[39] 49 C.F.R. § 376.12(c).
[40] Rediehs Express, Inc. v. Maple, 491 N.E.2d 1006 (Ind. 1986).
[41] Cosmopolitan Mutual Insurance Co. v. White, 336 F.Supp. 92 (D.Del. 1972).
[42] Kreider Truck Service, Inc. v. Augustine, 394 N.E.2d 1179 (Ill. 1979).

made every attempt to obtain the placards from the driver.[43] Under the theory of logo liability, the trucking company could be held liable for the driver's negligence if the placards remained on the vehicle even though the leased truck was not being driven on behalf of the company.[44]

In 1986, the provisions requiring the lessee motor carrier to remove the placards before terminating the lease were deleted, and instead the regulations allowed the lease to state which party would remove the identification markers from the vehicle.[45] Since this amendment, courts have shifted away from relying on a carrier's placards on a vehicle as determinative of the existence of a lease relationship and instead focused on the intent of the parties to the lease.[46] If the trucking company terminates the lease and attempts to retrieve its placards and a cancellation receipt from the owner but is unable to obtain them, then the company is no longer responsible for a driver's actions even though its placards are on the unit.[47] Although the existence of a carrier's placards on the truck is no longer determinative in defining the duration of the lease, the use of the placards is still evidence to be considered in determining if the lease was in effect at the time of the accident.[48] If a leased vehicle is under a permanent lease to one motor carrier but then a trip lease is executed to haul a load for another carrier, both carriers can be held responsible under the regulations governing lease liability.[49] The reason that the federal regulations place responsibility on the lessee motor carrier for the operation of the equipment is (1) to prevent carriers from avoiding safety regulations by the practice of leasing equipment from non-regulated carriers, (2) to promote highway safety by insuring that drivers furnished by exempt carriers as part of lease agreements do not violate safety regulations in the operation of the leased equipment, and (3) to provide shippers and other members of the public with financially responsible carriers.[50]

The current lease provisions in the federal regulations require an interstate carrier that leases a vehicle to (1) make the arrangement in writing signed by the parties specifying the duration and the compensation to be paid by the carrier, (2) carry a copy of the arrangement in each motor vehicle to which it applies during the period the arrangement is in effect, (3) inspect the motor vehicle and obtain liability and cargo insurance on it, and (4) have control of and be responsible for operating the vehicle in compliance with the federal regulations and other applicable laws as if the motor vehicle was owned by the carrier.[51] Although federal regulations require a written lease, the failure to have a written lease does not absolve a trucking company from liability if an oral lease exists.[52]

---

[43] Mellon National Bank & Trust Co. v. Sophie Lines, Inc., 289 F.2d 473 (3rd Cir. 1961); Kreider Truck Service, Inc. v. Augustine, 394 N.E.2d 1179 (1979).
[44] Rodriguez v. Ager, 705 F.2d 1229 (10th Cir. 1983).
[45] 49 C.F.R. § 376.12(c).
[46] Jackson v. O'Shields, 101 F.3d 1083 (5th Cir. 1996); PN Express, Inc. v. Zegel, 697 S.E.2d 226 (Ga. 2010); Amerigas Propane, L.P. v. Landstar Ranger, Inc., 184 Cal. App. 4th 981 (2010).
[47] Jackson v. O'Shields, 101 F.3d 1083 (5th Cir. 1996); Graham v. Malone Freight Lines, Inc., 948 F.Supp. 1124 (D.Mass. 1996).
[48] Williamson v. Steco Sales, Inc., 530 N.W.2d 412 (Wis. 1995); Davi ajbar, 266 A.D.2d 828 (N.Y. 1999).
[49] Simmons v. King, 478 F.2d 857 (5th Cir. 1973); Laux v. Juillerat, 680 F.Supp. 1131 (S.D. Ohio 1987); Zamalloa v. Hart, 31 F.3d 911 (9th Cir. 1994).
[50] Indiana Refrigerator Lines, Inc. v. Dalton, 516 F.2d 795 (6th Cir. 1975); Delaney v. Rapid Response, Inc., 81 F.Supp.3d 769 (2015).
[51] 49 U.S.C. § 14102(a).
[52] Wilson v. Riley Whittle, Inc., 701 P.2d 575 (Ariz. 1985); Fuller v. Reidel, 464 N.W.2d 97 (Wis. 1990); Zamalloa v. Hart, 31 F.3d 911 (9th Cir. 1994).

Owner/Operator Lease

INDEPENDENT CONTRACTOR OPERATING AGREEMENT

THIS AGREEMENT made this 11 day of April, 2015, between ▇▇▇▇▇▇▇▇, a corporation with its principal place of business in Jacksonville, Florida 32226 ("ACIS") and ▇▇▇▇▇▇▇▇, of ▇▇▇▇▇▇▇▇ ("Contractor").

RECITALS:

WHEREAS, ACIS, an interstate common and contract motor carrier of property, operates under Certificates of Public Convenience and Necessity issued by the Interstate Commerce Commission ("ICC") and wishes to perform the transportation of property with equipment ACIS does not own by contracting with independent owner/operators of transportation equipment; and

WHEREAS, the Contractor is engaged in the business of transporting freight by motor vehicle on behalf of, and pursuant to operating agreements with, private, contract or common carriers or shippers; and

WHEREAS, ACIS has entered into an Intermodal Freight Agency Agreement (the "Agency Agreement") with ▇▇▇▇▇▇▇▇ (the "Agent") pursuant to which Agent has agreed to perform certain services on behalf of ACIS, including but not limited to dispatching and compensating Contractors on behalf of ACIS either directly or indirectly through a third party payroll company; and

WHEREAS, it is to the mutual economic advantage of ACIS and the Contractor to enter into this Agreement for their pecuniary interest.

NOW, THEREFORE, in consideration of the mutual covenants, conditions and agreements contained herein, it is hereby agreed as follows:

1. **Contractor Equipment.** The Contractor represents and warrants to ACIS that the Contractor owns or has the right to use through valid and enforceable lease agreements the equipment more specifically described in Appendix "A" which by this reference is made a part hereof, together with drivers and all others necessary for labor, to spot equipment, to transport, load and unload freight on behalf of ACIS, or such certified carriers as ACIS may designate through authorized "Trip lease" agreements, as ACIS may, from time to time, make available to the Contractor. The Contractor represents and warrants that its drivers are trained, competent and qualified to perform truck driving services and that its equipment is in good, safe and efficient operating condition. The Contractor acknowledges and agrees that the Contractor's services shall be performed from ACIS's terminal located in ▇▇▇▇▇▇▇▇ (the "domiciled terminal"). ACIS shall exercise reasonable effort to make sufficient freight available so that the Contractor shall be able to keep the equipment in reasonably regular use under the terms of this Agreement, although this shall not be construed as an agreement by ACIS to furnish any specified number of loads or pounds of freight for transportation by the Contractor at any particular time or place.

2. **Compensation.** For the full and proper performance of the required services as more fully defined in paragraph 1 above, the Agent on behalf of ACIS agrees to pay the Contractor and the Contractor agrees that all compensation shall be due from Agent in accordance with the Compensation Addendum attached hereto and made a part hereof.

3. **Settlement.** Agent shall calculate and pay the compensation to the Contractor upon the submission by the Contractor or its agent by mail or in person those transportation documents showing full and proper performance of the terms of this Agreement. Compensation shall be payable by Agent to the Contractor on all authorized loads (as defined below) within fifteen (15) days of receipt by Agent at its principal office, or at such other place as Agent may designate, all documents that are or may be required by the ICC, the Department of Transportation ("DOT"), or Agent to bill its customers. These documents include but are not necessarily limited to signed, legible and properly completed delivery, loading/unloading records, drivers' logs, and accident reports, trip sheets, bills of lading, and any other receipts for which compensation is to be paid. For purposes of the Agreement, an "authorized load" is a load dispatched by Agent's dispatch or a trip leased or brokered load on which Agent's dispatch has issued a single trip lease release number to the Contractor for the load. That release number will be displayed on the trip sheet. Failure to display the release number on the appropriate trip sheet shall subject the Contractor to a One Hundred and no/100 Dollar ($100.00) deduction per load from any compensation due from Agent to the Contractor. Notwithstanding the foregoing, Agent shall have the right to deduct from any compensation otherwise due and payable to the Contractor hereunder any advances against compensation, cargo, personal injury or property damage claims; other costs specified in the Agreement; and any other Contractor expenses, costs, fines, or levies which Agent or ACIS may be required to pay, provided that Agent shall provide the Contractor a detailed description of any of such deductions. Amounts deducted for future or pending cargo, personal injury or property damage claims shall be placed in an escrow fund as hereinafter provided. If the Contractor is paid on a percentage basis, Agent will provide the Contractor with a copy of the rated freight bill, or a computer-generated document that contains the same information, at time of settlement. The Contractor shall, under any circumstance, be able to review ACIS's pertinent tariffs and documents underlying the computer-generated document at Agent's principal place of business DURING NORMAL BUSINESS HOURS.

4. **Regulatory compliance.** The Contractor recognizes that ACIS's business of providing motor carrier freight transportation service to the public is subject to regulation by the federal government acting through the ICC and the DOT and by various other federal, state and local governing bodies. Accordingly, the Contractor and its drivers and laborers shall be subject only to the limited control by Agent's dispatch and ACIS's safety department as is necessary to assure compliance with the laws and regulations imposed upon ACIS as a certified common and contract carrier.

The Contractor shall satisfy the following regulatory requirements:

A. Maintaining equipment in the state of repair required by all applicable regulations.

B. Operating the equipment in accordance with all applicable regulations.

C. Hiring only those drivers to operate the equipment who are qualified under all applicable federal and state laws, rules and regulations. Proof of driver qualifications will be provided ACIS before any driver is allowed to operate and will thereafter be re-certified to the Contractor on not less than an annual basis.

The entire lease is usually 4 to 5 pages and outlines responsibilities for insurance, maintenance and control of the vehicle and driver.

THEORIES OF LIABILITY

There is a split in authority as to whether a motor carrier may avoid liability for a driver's actions by showing that the driver was acting outside the scope of his agency relationship when a lease is in effect at the time of the accident.[53] Some jurisdictions hold that a trucking company is always responsible for a driver's operation of a leased vehicle for the duration of the lease.[54] Other jurisdictions hold that a rebuttable presumption of agency exists when a lease is in effect, and a motor carrier is only responsible for a driver's acts within the scope of his agency.[55]

The trucking company must be an authorized interstate motor carrier for lease liability to be applicable.[56] Although the vehicle owner who is not a motor carrier cannot be held liable for a driver's conduct under a theory of lease liability, the owner may always be held liable under common law theories of vicarious liability.[57] The mere presence of the carrier's logo on the side of a truck in a hit and run accident is not sufficient to hold the carrier responsible for the driver's actions without proof of a lease in effect at the time of the incident.[58] Applying a narrow interpretation of lease liability, a district court in Arkansas held that the owner of a tractor-trailer who contracted with a separate trucking company to drive the owner's vehicles using the owner's placards and interstate authority is not the statutory employer of the driver because the company was the statutory employer of the driver, and the owner did not exercise any control over the him.[59]

Passengers in leased vehicles are "members of the public" who are protected by the federal provisions governing a motor carrier's liability for the operation of a leased vehicle.[60] There is a split in authority as to whether drivers or co-employees in a leased vehicle are "members of the public" who are protected by the federal regulations. Some jurisdictions allow drivers and fellow employees to assert a cause of action against the trucking company as would any member of the public.[61] Other jurisdictions hold that drivers and co-employees are not intended beneficiaries of the federal regulatory scheme and cannot rely on lease provisions to bring an action against the lessee motor carrier.[62]

A manufacturer of goods which is not a motor carrier cannot be held liable for a driver's actions based on leasing a vehicle from a registered carrier where the manufacturer does not control the transportation process under the lease arrangement.[63] A trucking company is not responsible for the actions of a driver escorting an oversized load unless the escort driver is an agent and employee of the driver of the tractor-trailer unit.[64] The trucking company is not responsible for the conduct of the owner of the unit while the owner is repairing the vehicle in a warehouse or performing other functions outside of the lease agreement.[65] Lease liability provisions cannot be used to hold a lessor of trailers responsible for the conduct of the driver and trucking company since the lessor is not leasing

---

[53] Parker v. Erixon, 473 S.E.2d 421 (N.C. 1996).
[54] Baker v. Roberts Express, Inc., 800 F.Supp. 1571 (S.D. Ohio 1992); Wyckoff v. Marsh Bros. Trucking, 569 N.E.2d 1049 (Ohio 1991); Ryder Truck Rental Co., Inc. v. UTF Carriers, Inc., 719 F.Supp. 455 (W.D.Va. 1989); Planet Insurance Co. v. Transport Indemnity Co., 823 F.2d 285 (9th Cir. 1987); Harvey v. F-B Truck Line Co., 767 F.2d 254 (Id. 1987); Rodriguez v. Ager, 705 F.2d 1229 (10th Cir. 1983); Schedler v. Rowley Interstate Transportation Co., Inc., 368 N.E.2d 1287 (Ill. 1977); Simmons v. King, 478 F.2d 857 (5th Cir. 1973).
[55] Mensing v. Rochester Cheese Express, Inc., 423 N.W.2d 92 (Minn. 1988); Penn v. Virginia International Terminals, Inc., 819 F.Supp. 514 (E.D.Va. 1993); Wright v. Transus, Inc., 434 S.E.2d 786 (Ga. 1993); Parker v. Erixon, 473 S.E.2d 421 (N.C. 1996); Saullo v. Douglas, 957 So.2d 80 (Fla. 2007).
[56] Carroll v. Kamps, 2011 WL 2441503 (N.D. Ind. 2011); Castillo v. Gulf Coast Livestock Market, LLC, 392 S.W.3d 299 (Tx. 2012).
[57] Hiltgen v. Sumrall, 47 F.3d 695 (5th Cir. 1995).
[58] Thi v. Schneider National Carriers, Inc., 2005 WL 1703116 (W.D.Mo.).
[59] Brown v. Truck Connections International, Inc., 526 F.Supp.2d 920 (E.D.Ark. 2007).
[60] Price v. Westmoreland, 727 F.2d 494 (5th Cir. 1984); Powers v. Meyers, 655 N.E.2d 1358 (Ohio 1995).
[61] Proctor v. Colonial Refrigerated Transport, Inc., 494 F.2d 89 (4th Cir. 1974); Johnson v. S.O.S. Transport, Inc., 926 F.2d 516 (6th Cir. 1991); Smith v. Johnson, 862 F.Supp. 1287 (N.D.Pa. 1994).
[62] White v. Excalibur Insurance Co., 599 F.2d 50 (5th Cir. 1979), cert denied, 444 U.S. 965, 100 S.Ct. 452, 62 L.Ed.2d 377 (1979); Riddle v. Trans-Cold Express, Inc., 530 F.Supp. 186 (S.D.Ill. 1982); Coleman v. B-H Transfer Co., 659 S.E.2d 880 (Ga. 2008).
[63] LaPlant v. Cutlip, 258 A.2d 769 (N.Y. 1999).
[64] Brown v. Pettinari, 994 P.2d 1231 (Or. 2000); Kahrs v. Conley, 729 N.E.2d 191 (Ind. 2000).
[65] Zimprich v. Broekel, 519 N.W.2d 588 (N.D. 1994).

the vehicle for its own use and has given up possession to the lessee.[66] Lease The lease regulations do not render invalid indemnification agreements between carriers, and an owner may be required by contract to indemnify the trucking company for any loss caused by the owner's negligence.[67]

Practice Pointer: Request copies of any lease agreement related to the tractor or trailer.

C. Negligent Hiring, Entrustment or Retention

Negligent hiring involves the claim that the trucking company should not have hired the driver because the company should have known that the driver was incompetent at the time of his application for employment. Negligent entrustment is a slight variation on this theme and encompasses the allegation that the trucking company should not have entrusted a truck to the driver because of his inexperience or his inability to safely operate a commercial vehicle. Negligent retention occurs when a trucking company learns during the course of a driver's employment that the driver is incompetent but continues to retain the driver and allow him to operate a commercial vehicle.

A carrier has a duty to take steps to prevent injury to the driving public by determining the competency of its drivers to operate a commercial vehicle.[68] The FMCSA has created a database on truck drivers as part of its Pre-Employment Screening Process ("PSP"). A motor carrier may access a PSP report on a truck driver who has submitted a drivers application. The PSP report contains information on the results of the any audits, inspections or accidents involving the driver. The PSP report cannot be accessed by the public.

---

[66] Eisenberg v. Cope Bestway Express, Inc., 131 A.D. 3d. 1198 (2015).
[67] Transamerican Freight Lines, Inc. v. Brada Miller Freight Systems, Inc., 96 S.Ct. 229, 423 U.S. 28, 46 L.Ed.2d 169 (1975).
[68] Guidry v. National Freight, Inc., 944 S.W.2d 807 (Tx. 1997).

Truck Driver PSP Report

The PSP Report can identify a driver with a poor driving or inspection history.

Federal regulations outline a carrier's responsibilities to obtain background information on a driver before the carrier can hire him, and a failure to comply with these regulations will subject a carrier to a claim for negligent hiring if compliance would have identified the driver as incompetent.[69] If the driver fails to meet the minimum standards required by the federal regulations, then the trucking company can clearly be held liable for injuries resulting from the driver's operation of a commercial vehicle under a theory of negligent hiring or retention.[70] The real issue in most cases concerns the trucking company's liability for hiring a driver who has been involved in several prior accidents or has prior moving violations but is not disqualified from operating a commercial vehicle under the federal regulations. Whenever a trucking company hires or retains a driver who has more than one accident or moving violation, then the company exposes itself to potential liability for negligent hiring, entrustment or retention.[71] A trucking company is also responsible for negligent hiring if the company hires the driver in violation of its own policies and procedures concerning the number and severity of allowable traffic violations.[72] As such, a carrier exposes itself to potential liability for negligent hiring whenever it employs a driver who identifies past motor vehicle violations in his application for employment or whose violations are identified in the driver's moving violations report obtained from a State agency.[73] The trucking company may also be held responsible for negligent supervision or retention by failing to discipline or terminate a bad driver who commits offenses after he is hired by the company.[74] However, it is not sufficient to hold a company responsible for

---

[69] Wallen v. Allen, 343 S.E.2d 73 (Va. 1986).
[70] Lakes v. Minor, 620 N.E.2d 1015 (Ohio 1993); TXI Transportation Co. v. Hughes, 224 S.W.3d 970 (Tx. 2007).
[71] Boyd v. L.G. DeWitt Trucking Co., Inc., 405 S.E.2d 914 (N.C. 1991).
[72] Morris v. JTM Materials, Inc., 78 S.W.3d 28 (Tx. 2002).
[73] Boyd v. L.G. DeWitt Trucking Co., Inc., 405 S.E.2d 914 (N.C. 1991); But see Ghimbasan v. S&H Express, Inc., 814 F.Supp.2d 120 (Ct. 2011) (Refusing to recognize a tort for negligent entrustment).
[74] Frederick v. Swift Transportation Co., 616 F.3d 1074 (10th Cir. 2010).

negligently hiring or retaining a driver when the driver does not have a pattern of bad driving and just has one or two minor traffic violations.[75]

If the trucking company fails to investigate the driver's qualifications as required by the regulations, the company is deemed to have knowledge not only of the violations and accidents disclosed to it, but also of any facts about the driver's history which would have been revealed had the company performed the appropriate background checks.[76] This doctrine of imputed knowledge keeps the company from being rewarded for its failure to discover a driver's record when it has a duty to obtain this information.[77] If the driver does not have a bad driving history and an appropriate background check would have shown nothing, then the failure to conduct a background check cannot be the cause of the collision and is not a basis for liability.[78] There are numerous services that provide background checks on drivers, including USIS and HireRight.

---

[75] Craft v. Triumph Logistics, 107 F.Supp.3d 1218 (M.D. Ala. 2015); McCutchen v. Valley Home, Inc., 100 F.Supp.3d 1235 (N.D. Ala. 2015).
[76] Smith v. Tommy Roberts Trucking Co., 435 S.E.2d 54, 57 (1993).
[77] Id. at 57.
[78] Moore Freight Services, 545 S.W. 3d 85 (Tx. 2017).

USIS Report

Transportation Employment History

```
Customer Name:           ███████████ (50012)            130394735
Actor Name:              ███████████ ()
Customer Reference:
Customer Sub:
================================================================
                    EMPLOYMENT HISTORY #1
----------------------------------------------------------------
Search using ███████████████████████
----------------------------------------------------------------
              EMPLOYMENT RECORD   07/26/2010  14:29:31   4500964303

Driver:         ███████████       SSN: ████████    DOB: ████████

Contributed By: Werner Enterprises            Phone: (402)895-6640
                14507 FRONTIER RD
                OMAHA, NE 68137

    Original data received by DAC on 07/20/2006

        Period of Service:       From 07/2006 To 07/2006
        License Number:          ████████
        ELIGIBLE FOR REHIRE:     Review required before rehiring
        REASON FOR LEAVING:      Discharged (or Company Terminated Lease)
        STATUS:                  Student/Trainee
        DRIVER'S EXPERIENCE:     Over the Road
        EQUIPMENT OPERATED:      Dry Box
        LOADS HAULED:            Gen. Commodity

----------------------------------------------------------------
                    Accident/Incident Record

Equipment was involved in an occurrence or act that produced unintended injury,
death, property damage of any type, or resulted in the equipment requiring a
tow (other than mechanical breakdown) while assigned to the driver regardless
of fault. Adverse information is reported for 7 years.

   Number of DOT Recordable accidents less than 7 years old: 0
   Number of Non DOT Recordable Accidents/Incidents less than 7 years old: 0

No additional accident/incident information available.
================================================================


================================================================
                    EMPLOYMENT HISTORY #2
----------------------------------------------------------------
Search using ███████████████████████
----------------------------------------------------------------
              EMPLOYMENT RECORD   07/26/2010  14:29:31   4500364103

Driver:         ███████████       SSN: ████████    DOB: None on file

Contributed By: Digby Truck Lines Inc         Phone: (800)873-4429
```

The background report may include a driving history, criminal background check and employment history.

In addition, as part of the CSA system, the FMCSA keeps a database on truck drivers that includes the result of any inspections, audits or accidents involving the driver.

A commercial vehicle driver is disqualified for various lengths of time for serious traffic violations.[79] Under this comprehensive scheme, drivers are disqualified from operating a commercial vehicle for 60 days for any second conviction within a three year period of any combination of any offense committed in a commercial vehicle of (1) speeding in excess of 15 mph over the speed limit, (2) driving recklessly, (3) making improper or erratic lane changes, (4) following the vehicle ahead too closely, (5) violating any motor vehicle traffic control law arising in connection with a fatal accident, (6) texting while driving or (7) driving without a commercial driver's license.[80]

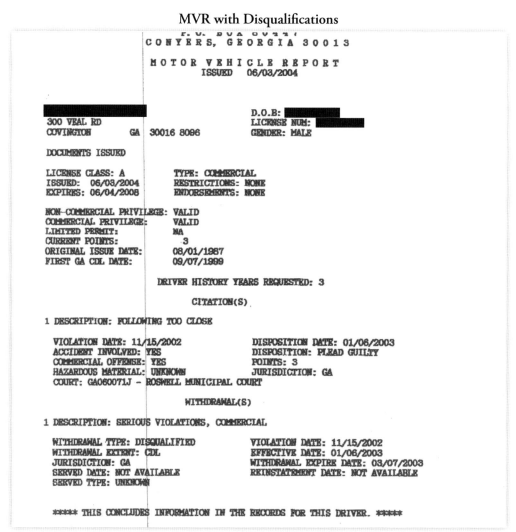

In this case, we discovered that the defendant driver's license was suspended at the time of the accident because of his prior traffic violations.

A driver is disqualified for one year for driving under the influence of alcohol or controlled substances or leaving the scene of an accident, whether the offense occurs in a commercial vehicle or a non-commercial vehicle.[81] A driver is also disqualified for a year if he continues to operate a

---

[79] 49 C.F.R. § 383.51.
[80] 49 C.F.R. § 383.51.
[81] 49 C.F.R. § 383.51.

commercial vehicle after having been disqualified.[82] Motor carriers have an obligation to monitor their drivers for any disqualifying offenses,[83] and these new provisions give additional grounds for negligent hiring and retention claims.

Negligent hiring, entrustment or retention claims are causes of action based on a trucking company's direct negligence in employing an incompetent driver rather than on vicarious liability for the driver's actions.[84] The company's liability is not dependent upon a finding that the driver was acting within the scope of his employment when the tortious act occurred.[85] Most jurisdictions will not allow a plaintiff to bring claims for negligent hiring and retention when the trucking company admits an agency relationship with the driver.[86] The basis for this rule is that a company's admission of agency establishes the liability link from the negligence of the driver to the carrier rendering proof of negligent hiring and retention unnecessary and irrelevant.[87] An exception to this general rule exists when the plaintiff asserts a separate claim for punitive damages based on the issues of negligent hiring and retention.[88] In this situation, evidence of negligent hiring and retention can be presented to the jury as a basis for an award of punitive damages.[89]

While a trucking company clearly has a duty to investigate the driving experience and qualifications of a driver, most jurisdictions have held that the company does not have a duty to investigate the driver's non-vehicular criminal background.[90] Because drivers are hired to transport freight and not to interact with the public as the company's representative, a trucking company does not have to perform an independent investigation into a driver's criminal past to determine if he is a violent individual who may attack or sexually assault a person.[91] It would also be cost-prohibitive for a trucking company to conduct a criminal search on each driver since the company would have to review court records from every jurisdiction with which the driver had any significant contacts to complete the search.[92] Accordingly, a trucking company cannot usually be held responsible under a negligent hiring or retention theory for an intentional assault inflicted by a driver.[93]

Practice Pointer: Conduct discovery on the issues of negligent hiring and retention by requesting relevant documents and deposing the company's safety director. If there is evidence of negligent hiring and retention, amend the complaint to add these claims and a punitive damages claim based on the hiring of the driver to avoid any chance of having the claims dismissed if the company admits agency.

D. Actions against Insurers for Negligent Hiring

Insurance companies are playing a larger role in the hiring process of new drivers for small trucking companies. Instead of making an independent assessment of a driver's qualifications, small trucking companies rely on their insurance company to make this decision for them. The trucking company obtains the necessary information from the new applicant and then submits

---

[82] 49 C.F.R. § 383.51.
[83] 49 C.F.R. § 383.51(a).
[84] Boyd v. L.G. DeWitt Trucking Co., Inc., 405 S.E.2d 914 (N.C. 1991).
[85] Morris at 14.
[86] Cole v. Alton, 567 F.Supp. 1084 (N.D. Miss. 1983); Bartja v. National Union Fire Insurance Co. of Pittsburgh, PA, 463 S.E.2d 358 (Ga. 1996); McHaffie v. Bunch, 891 S.W.3d 822 Mo. 1995); Lee v. J.B. Hunt Transport, Inc., 308 F.Supp.2d 310 (S.D.N.Y. 2004).
[87] Bartja at 361.
[88] Smith at 57.
[89] Id. at 57.
[90] Connes v. Molalla Transport System, Inc., 831 P.2d 1316 (Col. 1992); C.C. v. Roadrunner Trucking, Inc., 823 F.Supp. 913 (D.Utah 1993); Guidry v. National Freight, Inc., 944 S.W.2d 807 (Tx. 1997); Carberry v. Golden Hawk Transport Co., 402 S.W.3d 556 (Ky. 2013).
[91] Connes at 1321-1322. But compare, Malorney v. B&L Motor Freight, Inc., 496 N.E.2d 1086 (Ill. 1986) (Because trucking company did not present any evidence that it would be unduly burdensome to conduct criminal background checks on its drivers, company can be held responsible for failing to discover that driver who raped hitchhiker had long history of sexual crimes).
[92] C.C. at 924.
[93] Id.

the information to the insurance company. The insurance company reviews the information and then determines if the insurer will provide coverage for the new applicant. The trucking company's decision to hire the driver is based entirely on the "insurability" of the driver. In effect, the insurer is screening new drivers for the trucking company and making the decision as to whether to hire the driver. Although the insurer has no duty under state or federal law to screen drivers, the insurer may be held responsible for negligently undertaking this duty if the insurer fails to reject an unqualified or incompetent driver.[94] However, an insurer has no obligation to make sure that a motor carrier is fit to operate as a trucking company before issuing them an insurance policy as long as the insurer does not undertake to participate in the hiring of drivers.[95]

Practice Pointer: If the trucking company is a small business and there is not sufficient liability coverage for the plaintiff's injuries, examine the relationship between the insurer and motor carrier to determine if the insurer controlled the screening of new drivers.

E.   Broker Liability

A broker is an entity that does not transport the load but deals with the shipper and motor carrier in arranging the transportation.[96] A broker is often the "middle man" between the shipper and motor carrier. Traditionally, the broker has avoided liability for any injuries caused by the driver transporting the load by demonstrating that the motor carrier was an independent contractor.[97] Because the broker is not the employer of the driver, it cannot be held liable under a theory of agency or vicarious liability.[98] However, when the broker controls the manner and method of work and has the ability to fine or discipline the truck driver, then a jury issue exists as to whether the driver is the broker's agent.[99]

The broker may also be held liable under a negligent hiring theory if the broker did not properly screen the motor carrier and failed to investigate the carrier's safety record.[100] Prior to hiring a motor carrier to transport a load, a broker must at a minimum check the general safety statistics and evaluations of the carrier and review any internal records of the carrier's safety performance.[101] If a motor carrier has a "conditional" safety rating or borderline safety history reflected in its SMS results, the broker has a duty to investigate further to make sure the motor carrier is operating safely on the public roads.[102] A failure to properly evaluate a carrier's safety record will subject the broker to liability for negligent hiring.[103] However, a broker is not responsible for the trucking company hiring an unsafe driver if the broker did not know about the driver, and the trucking company itself appeared to be safe based on FMCSA data.[104]

Practice Pointer: Determine if a broker was involved in arranging the transportation and if the broker checked the motor carrier's safety record.

---

[94] Osowski v. Smith, 586 S.E.2d 71 (Ga. 2003).
[95] Salazar v. Ramos, 361 S.W.3d 739 (Tx. 2012).
[96] 49 U.S.C. § 13102(2).
[97] Graham v. Malone Freight Lines, Inc., 314 F.3d 7 (1st Cir. 1999); Kavulak v. Laimis Juodzevicius, A.V., Inc., 994 F.Supp.2d 337 (W.D.N.Y. 2014); Harris v. Fedex National LTL, Inc., 760 F.3d 780 (8th Cir. 2014); Hayward v. C.H. Robinson Co., Inc., 24 N.E.3d 48 (Ill. 2014).
[98] Schramm v. Foster, 341 F.Supp.2d 536, 545 (Md. 2004); Jones v. C.H. Robinson Worldwide, Inc., 558 F.Supp.2d 630 (W.D.Va. 2008).
[99] Sperl v. C.H. Robinson Worldwide, Inc., 946 N.E.2d 463 (Ill. 2011).
[100] Schramm. at 551.
[101] Id.
[102] Jones v. C.H. Robinson Worldwide, Inc., 558 F.Supp.2d 630 (W.D.Va. 2008).
[103] Id.
[104] McLaine v. McLeod, 661 S.E.2d 695 (Ga. 2008).

F. Negligent Inspection, Maintenance or Repair

Many accidents are attributable to mechanical failures of parts or systems in a commercial vehicle. Federal regulations require motor carriers to systematically inspect, maintain, and repair all motor vehicles subject to their control.[105] The regulations also provide that all parts and accessories on a commercial vehicle must be kept in safe and proper operating condition at all times.[106] A trucking company must maintain the following records for each vehicle under its control: (1) the identification of the owner and style of the vehicle, (2) a list of the nature and due date of various inspection and maintenance operations to be performed on the vehicle, and (3) a record of inspection, repairs and maintenance performed on the vehicle.[107] These records must be maintained for one year while the vehicle is either housed or maintained by the carrier and for six months after the motor vehicle leaves the carrier's control.[108] A motor carrier can be held responsible for any injury caused by its failure to properly inspect, maintain or repair any equipment in its control.[109] For example, if the brakes are discovered to be out of adjustment after an accident, the trucking company can be found liable for failing to properly conduct a pre-trip inspection and failing to properly adjust the brakes to keep them within the federal limits.[110] The prior owner of a tractor trailer who sells the vehicle to another trucking company can be held responsible for negligent maintenance of the vehicle in violation of the FMCSR when the mechanical condition resulted in an accident.[111]

Practice Pointer: Have a qualified trucking expert conduct an inspection of the vehicle as soon as possible after the accident to determine if mechanical problems played any role in the accident and obtain a copy of any post-accident DOT, PSC or FHWA inspection of the vehicle.

G. Violations of the Federal Motor Carrier Safety Regulations ("FMCSR")

The FMCSR are a comprehensive list of guidelines and specifications governing the operation and maintenance of commercial vehicles. Every interstate motor carrier is required to be knowledgeable of and comply with all the provisions of the FMCSR applicable to that motor carrier's operations.[112] Every driver and employee must be instructed regarding compliance with the FMCSR.[113] Equipment and accessories required by the regulations must be maintained in compliance with all applicable performance and design criteria.[114] No person may aid, abet, encourage or require a motor carrier or its drivers to violate any safety regulation.[115] A trucking company can be held liable for any injury resulting from its violation an applicable provision of the FMCSR.[116] An intrastate carrier or an entity transporting an exempt commodity may not be held liable for injuries resulting from an accident based on a violation of the FMCSR but may be held liable under common law theories of negligence.[117] As with other federal regulations, agencies in most states have adopted the provisions of the FMCSR as applicable to any commercial vehicles operated within the state.[118]

Practice Pointer: Review the FMCSR to determine if the driver or company violated any federal regulations.

---

[105] 49 C.F.R. § 396.3(a).
[106] 49 C.F.R. § 396.3(a)(1).
[107] 49 C.F.R. § 396.3(b).
[108] 49 C.F.R. § 396.3(c).
[109] Lynden Transport, Inc. v. Haragan, 623 P.2d 789 (Alaska 1981); Knight v. Schneider National Carriers, Inc., 350 F.Supp.2d 775 (N.D. Ill. 2004).
[110] Indian Trucking v. Harber, 752 N.E.2d 168 (Ind. 2001).
[111] Bailey v. Lewis Farm, Inc., 171 P.3d 336 (Ore. 2007).
[112] 49 C.F.R. § 390.3(e)(1).
[113] 49 C.F.R. § 390.3(e)(2).
[114] 49 C.F.R. § 390.3(e)(3).
[115] 49 C.F.R. § 390.13.
[116] Hageman v. TSI, Inc., 786 P.2d 452 (Col. 1989).
[117] Disidore v. Mail Contractors of America, Inc., 2001 WL 506838 (D. Kan. 2001); Stanley v. Fiber Transport, Inc., 470 S.E.2d 767 (Ga. 1996).
[118] See Transportation Rules of the Georgia Public Service Commission.

H. FMCSR Violations by Vehicles Smaller than a Tractor Trailer

The FMCSR applies to all commercial vehicles.[119] A commercial vehicle is defined as any vehicle used on the highway in interstate commerce transporting people or property with a gross vehicle weight rating (GVWR) or gross combination weight rating or gross vehicle weight rating or gross combination weight of 10,001 lbs. or more.[120] Transporting property means carrying any tools or equipment as part of a commercial enterprise.[121] Most states have adopted the FMCSR and its definition of a commercial vehicle as applicable to any vehicles involved in intrastate commerce. The end result is that the owner and/or operator of any business vehicle and/or trailer with any load which in combination weighs more than 10,001 lbs. must comply with all the FMCSR. Straight trucks, work vans, large pickup trucks with trailers, landscaping vehicles, HVAC work vehicles, plumbing trucks and utility trucks may fall within this definition of a commercial vehicle. Many of the owners and operators of these vehicles have no idea that they have to follow the FMCSR. In this situation, not only would the violations of the FMCSR result in liability for the owner, but the ignorance of the regulations would likely also result in punitive damages.

Work Vehicle Meeting Definition of Commercial Vehicle

**Practice Pointer: If you have a case with a vehicle smaller than a tractor trailer, look at the weight of the vehicle, trailer and any equipment to see if it meets the definition of a commercial vehicle.

I. Shipper Liability

Similar to a broker, a shipper may be held responsible for a driver's actions if the shipper maintains control of the method and manner of the delivery process and can discipline the driver[122] or if the shipper fails to look at the qualifications of the trucking company and the trucking company was clearly incompetent and unsafe.[123] The shipper may also be held liable if the accident was related to improper loading of the vehicle. Under this theory of liability, a shipper who participates in the loading process is responsible under a common law theory of negligence for failing to properly secure

---

[119] 49 C.F.R. § 390.3.
[120] 49 C.F.R. § 390.5.
[121] Midwest Crane and Rigging, Inc. v. FMCSA, 603 F.3d 837 (10th Cir. 2010); Friedrich v. U.S. Computer Services, 974 F.2d 409 (3rd Cir. 1992).
[122] Caroll v. Kamps, 795 F.Supp.2d 794 (N.D. 2011); Ramirez v. Garcia, 413 S.W.3d 134 (Tx. 2013); Harris v. Fedex National LTL, Inc., 760 F.3d 780 (8th Cir. 2014); Gonzalez v. Ramirez, 463 S.W.3d 499 (Tx. 2015).
[123] McComb v. Bugarin, 20 F.Supp.3d 676 (N.D.Ill. 2014).

the load.[124] Although the basis of recovery is common law negligence, the FMCSR provides evidence of the applicable standard of care.[125] If the trailer is sealed before it is picked up by the motor carrier, it is presumed that the shipper participated in the loading process.[126]

The shipper may also be held liable for the driver's conduct if the shipper retains control over the transportation process.[127] If the motor carrier is an independent contractor with the shipper, the shipper can be held responsible for negligent hiring if the shipper fails to investigate the minimum qualifications of the motor carrier on the issues of licensing, registration and insurance.[128] A shipper is not liable for a driver's actions simply by obtaining an oversized load permit for the shipment.[129]

**Practice Pointer: If the accident involved a load shift, overweight vehicle or improperly secured load, consider an action against the shipper for negligently loading the vehicle.

J. Driver Fatigue

Many commercial vehicle accidents are caused by a driver's inattentiveness or fatigue resulting from the operation of a vehicle for an excessive amount of time. Federal regulations prohibit a trucking company from allowing a driver to operate a commercial vehicle while the driver's ability or alertness is impaired by fatigue, illness, or any other cause which would make it unsafe for the driver to operate the commercial vehicle.[130] These regulations also prescribe a maximum number of hours that a driver can be on duty during any day or week and require a driver to maintain a log of his work status.[131] Under the federal regulations, the motor carrier is now required to have an electronic log system through a GPS on-board recording system in the vehicle that records the duty status of the driver.[132]

---

[124] Burke v. J.F. Allen Co., 182 F.3d 907 (W.Va. 1999); Skeie v. Mercer Trucking Co., Inc., 61 P.3d 1207 (Wash. 2003); Bujnoch v. National Oilwell Barco, L.P., 542 S.W.3d 2 (Tx. 2018).
[125] Reed v. Ace Doran Hauling & Rigging Co., 1997 WL 177849 (N.D. Ill. 1997); Symington v. Great Western Trucking Co., Inc., 668 F.Supp. 1278 (S.D.Iowa 1987); Locicero v. Interpace Corp., 266 N.W.2d 423 (Wis. 1978).
[126] Miller v. Rollins Leasing Corp., 1999 WL 739539 (Ohio 1999).
[127] Detrick v. Midwest Pipe & Steel, Inc., 598 N.E.2d 1074 (Ind. 1992).
[128] Puckrein v. ATI Transport, Inc., 897 A.2d 1034 (N.J. 2006).
[129] Fike v. Peace, 964 So.2d 651 (Ala. 2007).
[130] 49 C.F.R. § 392.3.
[131] 49 C.F.R. § 395 et. seq.
[132] 49 C.F.R. § 395.8.

Electronic Log

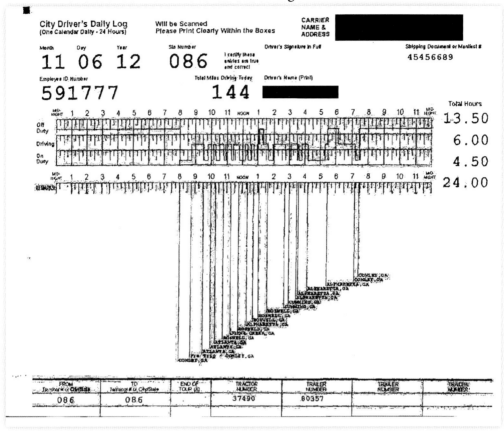

This log is automatically generated by the on-board computer system.

The only time that a driver can use a hand-written log is if the driver is part-time or the vehicle was manufactured before 2000.[133]

---

[133] 49 C.F.R. § 395.8.

Handwritten Driver's Log

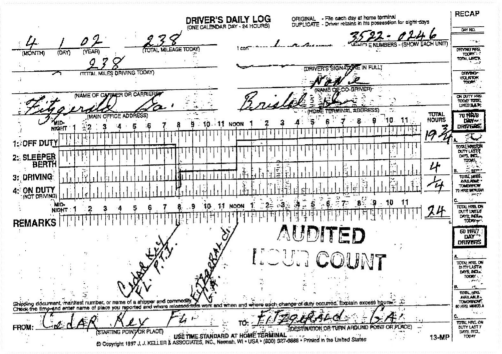

The Driver's Log must be kept in one time zone which is usually the home state of the driver.

A carrier has a duty to monitor its driver's logs through an appropriate log verification procedure and to establish proper controls of driving time to ensure compliance with maximum hours of service regulations.[134] The purpose of these regulations is to prevent accidents caused by driver fatigue, and any violation of these requirements is admissible to prove negligence for a subsequent accident.[135] Courts will usually not allow a plaintiff to proceed under a theory of liability based on violations of the maximum hours requirements or driver's logs provisions if there is no evidence that the accident was related to driver inattentiveness or fatigue.[136]

**Practice Pointer: Retain a qualified expert to examine the trucking company's system of monitoring its drivers' hours of service.

K. Commercial Driver's License ("CDL") Manual

Each state has its own CDL Manual that outlines the proper manner in which to drive a commercial vehicle. These manuals are remarkably similar from state to state. A commercial driver should be familiar with the requirements contained in the CDL Manual of the state in which he has his license. These manuals establish industry standards for the truck driver and company. There are usually sections on basic truck safety such as Space Management, Controlling Speed, and Seeing Hazards and sections tailored to specific circumstances like Night Driving, Driving in Fog and Skid Control and Recovery. The driver will be in violation of industry standards if he violated any of the provisions contained in the CDL Manual.[137]

---

[134] Torres v. North American Van Lines, Inc., 658 P.2d 835 (Ariz. 1982).
[135] NeSmith v. Bowden, 563 P.2d 1322 (Wash. 1977); Greist v. Phillips, 906 P.2d 789 (Or. 1995).
[136] Smith v. Printup, 938 P.2d 1261 (Kan. 1997); Burke v. Maassen, 904 F.2d 178 (3rd Cir. 1990).
[137] Schultz v. Lester, 2011 WL 3211271 (Tx. 2011); Langille v. Transco, Inc., 2013 WL 6185347 (D.Wy. 2013).

Georgia CDL Manual

2009
GEORGIA
COMMERCIAL DRIVER'S MANUAL

We have used the Georgia CDL Manual at trial to cross-examine a commercial driver on improper maneuvers.

L. Driver Distraction

There are numerous driver distractions within and around the tractor that can lead to an accident if a truck driver takes his eyes off the roadway. Most CDL manuals have a warning about driver distractions.

2.9.1 – Don't Drive Distracted
If drivers react a half-second slower because of distractions, crashes double. Some tips to follow so you won't become distracted:

Review and be totally familiar with all safety and usage features on any in-vehicle electronics, including your wireless or cell phone, before you drive.
Pre-program radio stations.
Pre-load you favorite CDs or cassette tapes.
Clear the vehicle of any unnecessary objects.
Review maps and plan your route before you begin driving.
Adjust all mirrors for best all-round visibility before you start your trip.
Don't attempt to read or write while you drive.
Avoid smoking, eating and drinking while you drive.
Don't engage in complex or emotionally intense conversations with other occupants.

2.9.2 – Use In-vehicle Communication Equipment Cautiously

When possible, pull off the road in a safe, legal place when making/receiving a call on communication equipment.
If possible, turn the cell phone off until your destination is reached.
Position the cell phone within easy reach.
Pre-program cell phones with commonly called numbers.
If you have to place a call, find a safe place to pull off the road. Do not place a call while driving.
Some jurisdictions require that only hands-free devices can be used while driving. Even these devices are unsafe to use when you are moving down the road.
If you must use your cell phone, keep conversations short. Develop ways to get free of long-winded friends and associates while on the road. Never use the cell phone for social visiting.
Hang up in tricky traffic situations.
Do not use the equipment when approaching locations with heavy traffic, road construction, heavy pedestrian traffic, or severe weather conditions.
Do not attempt to type or read messages on your satellite system while driving.

The two main driver distractions that have received most of the publicity in the news is use of cellphones and on-board computer messaging systems. The FMCSA prohibits any texting while driving.[138] Texting is defined as any "electronic text retrieval or entry, short message service, emailing, instant messaging, accessing the internet, or pressing more than a single button to make a or receive a call."[139] Regulations also require a truck driver to use a hands-free cellphone while driving.[140] Most CDL manuals warn against using cellphones in any manner while driving a commercial vehicle.

If the truck driver was talking on his cellphone or texting while driving, it can constitute negligence and could have contributed to the cause of the accident. However, there does not appear to be a product liability claim against the manufacturer of the texting device for allowing the truck driver to text while driving.[141]

**Practice Pointer: Always subpoena copies of the truck driver's cellphone records to see if he was texting or talking on the cellphone at the time of the incident.

M. Co-Driver Situations Involving Leased Drivers

Trucking companies that carry expedited loads or have numerous cross-country deliveries often rely on co-driver situations to transport freight in a non-stop manner. One driver will be operating the vehicle while the other driver is asleep in the sleeper berth. The drivers will then switch positions every 12 hours. In this manner, the vehicle is always in operation without violating any hours of service regulations. Many times these co-drivers are leased to the company instead of being company drivers in order to avoid the need for the trucking company to purchase workers compensation

---

[138] 49 C.F.R. § 392.80.
[139] 49 C.F.R. § 390.5.
[140] 49 C.F.R. § 392.82.
[141] Durkee v. C.H. Robinson Worldwide, Inc., 765 F.Supp.2d 742 (W.D.N.C. 2011).

coverage for the drivers. In this scenario, if there is an accident caused by the negligence of the truck driver, the co-driver would have a claim against the driver and the trucking company for any injuries suffered in the collision.[142] While claims involving co-employees are usually barred by worker's compensation immunity, this is not the case in a co-driver situation where the drivers are both leased to the company because they are not employees of the trucking company for workers compensation purposes.[143]

**Practice Pointer: If you have a case where a co-driver has been injured in an accident, you should look at the possibility of bringing a lawsuit against the trucking company.

N. Spoliation of Evidence

Federal regulations require interstate carriers to maintain and preserve records for various lengths of time.[144] After an accident, a carrier will often destroy pertinent records, either purposefully or in the ordinary course of its document retention procedures. The destruction of documents, often referred to as spoliation, can lead to sanctions against the trucking company.[145] As a sanction for spoliation of evidence by a party to an action, a court may (1) charge the jury that spoliation of evidence creates the rebuttable presumption that the evidence would have been harmful to the spoliator, (2) exclude any testimony about the evidence, or (3) enter judgment against the party which tampered with the evidence.[146] The severity of the sanction must be determined according to (1) whether the party seeking sanctions was prejudiced as a result of the destruction of the evidence, (2) whether the prejudice can be cured, (3) the importance of the evidence, (4) whether the party who destroyed the evidence acted in bad faith, and (5) the potential for abuse if expert testimony about the evidence is not excluded.[147] A few jurisdictions even recognize a separate cause of action for spoliation of evidence.[148] These jurisdictions have set forth the element of the tort as (1) the existence of pending or probable litigation involving the plaintiff, (2) defendant's knowledge of the pendency or fact of the litigation, (3) destruction of evidence by the defendant designed to disrupt the plaintiff's case, (4) disruption of the plaintiff's case, and (5) damages proximately caused by the defendant's acts.[149]

The driving force behind imposing sanctions for spoliation is the concept that it is unfair to have a plaintiff's case adversely affected by the trucking company's failure to preserve and maintain relevant evidence. The company will usually argue that the destruction of the evidence was inadvertent and that the evidence would have been preserved if it had only known that it was relevant to plaintiff's case. The solution to this problem is to send a spoliation letter by certified mail to the trucking company and its representatives as early in the litigation as possible. A sample spoliation letter can be found in the Appendix, XVIII-1.

A standard spoliation letter lists in detail certain items of evidence which are to be "maintained and preserved" and not be "destroyed, discarded, changed, repaired, or altered in any manner." The letter states that this evidence is relevant to the plaintiff's cause of action and that the plaintiff will seek all sanctions allowed under the law if the evidence is destroyed. Once the spoliation letter is received, the motor carrier is on notice of the relevance of the listed items and must take affirmative steps to maintain and preserve this evidence or risk the imposition of harsh sanctions. Because of ethical considerations concerning direct contact with opposing parties, an attorney should always

---

[142] Proctor v. Colonial Refrigerated Transportation, Inc., 494 F.2d 89 (4th Cir. 1973); Wilkerson v. Allied Van Lines, Inc., 521 A.2d 25 (1987); Johnson v. S.O.S. Transport, 926 F.2d 516 (6th Cir. 1991); Simpson v. Empire Truck Lines, 571 F.3d 475 (5th Cir. 2009); Vargas v. FMI, Inc., 233 Cal. App. 4th 638 (2015).
[143] Simpson v. Empire Truck Lines, 571 F.3d 475 (5th Cir. 2009).
[144] 49 C.F.R. Pt. 379, App. A.; Record Retention Checklist, Trucking Checklists 4.
[145] R.A. Siegel Co. v. Bowen, 539 S.E.2d 873 (Ga. 2000); Ogin v. Ahmed, 563 F.Supp.2d 539 (M.D.Penn. 2008).
[146] Chapman v. Auto Owners Insurance Co., 469 S.E.2d 783 (Ga. 1996).
[147] Id. at 783.
[148] Hazen v. Municipality of Anchorage, 718 P.2d 456 (Alaska 1986); Smith v. Howard Johnson Co., 615 N.E.2d 1037 (Ohio 1993); Coleman v. Eddy Potash, Inc., 905 P.2d 185 (N.M. 1995) Guillory v. Dillard's Department Store, Inc., 777 So.2d 1 (La. 2000); Smith v. Atkinson, 771 So.2d 429 (Ala. 2000).
[149] Rosenblit v. Zimmerman, 766 A.2d 749 (N.J. 2001).

review State Bar rules and regulations to make sure the content of his spoliation letter is consistent with any ethical requirements.

Federal regulations designate the amount of time that most records must be maintained.[150] Trucking companies must exercise reasonable care in choosing retention periods for records that do not have a specific period of time designated in the federal regulations, and the choice of retention periods shall reflect past experiences, company needs, pending litigation, and regulatory requirements.[151] States and other governmental entities may prescribe longer retention periods for any category of records.[152] A carrier may destroy any records at its discretion after the required retention period expires.[153] Records may be maintained by any technology that is immune to alteration, modification or erasure of the underlying data and will enable production of an accurate and unaltered paper copy.[154]

Practice Pointer: Send a spoliation letter as soon as possible to place the trucking company on notice as to the importance of maintaining and preserving all relevant documents.

O. Punitive Damages

Punitive damages are only warranted when the conduct of the trucking company amounts to more than just negligence and instead demonstrates recklessness or a want of care for the consequences of its actions.[155] In many jurisdictions, a plaintiff can recover punitive damages against a company when the driver's actions are reckless or wanton under the same guidelines for imputing responsibility for a driver's negligence.[156] In these jurisdictions, the motor carrier is liable for any award of punitive damages based on the driver's misconduct, i.e., when the driver operates a vehicle under the influence of alcohol or drugs or drives a vehicle with known mechanical problems.[157] The trucking company may be held directly liable for punitive damages if the driver's history is so egregious as to make the hiring or retention of the driver amount to reckless conduct on behalf of the company.[158] The company can also be held directly responsible for punitive damages if it has a common practice of ignoring federal regulations or failing to monitor its drivers,[159] or if it destroys documents to hide any potential violations.[160]

Practice Pointer: Retain a qualified expert to determine if the trucking company is complying with its obligations to monitor drivers under the federal regulations.

---

[150] 49 C.F.R. § 379 et. seq.
[151] 49 C.F.R. Pt. 379, App. A, Note A.
[152] 49 C.F.R. § 379.3.
[153] 49 C.F.R. § 379.3.
[154] 49 C.F.R. § 379.7(a).
[155] See O.C.G.A. § 51-12-5.1.
[156] Phillips v. Dallas Carrier Corp., 766 F.Supp. 416 (M.D.N.C. 1991).
[157] Id. at 419-420.
[158] Smith v. Tommy Roberts Trucking Co., 435 S.E.2d 54 (Ga. 1993).
[159] Torres v. North American Van Lines, Inc., 658 P.2d 835 (Ariz. 1982); Burke v. TransAm Trucking, Inc., 605 F.Supp.2d 647 (M.D. Penn. 2009).
[160] J.B. Hunt Transport, Inc. v. Bentley, 427 S.E.2d 429 (Ga. 1993).

III. Federal Regulations Governing Driver Qualifications

A. Pre-Employment Screening

Federal regulations require an interstate motor carrier to obtain certain background information on a driver before hiring him.[161] Most jurisdictions, through rules issued by a state Public Service Commission or a similar entity, have adopted the federal regulations as guidelines for intrastate carriers to complete the same background checks.[162] Under the federal regulatory scheme, a driver applying for employment with a trucking company must complete a comprehensive application listing any moving violations or accidents for the three-year period prior to the date of the application and identifying each motor carrier for whom the driver has worked for the past ten years.[163]

Driver's Application

A Driver's Application is usually 4 to 5 pages and may include additional handouts which must be signed by the driver.

Within thirty days of hiring a driver, the trucking company must make inquiries with the driver's prior employers for the three-year period prior to the date of his employment and must obtain a

---

[161] 49 C.F.R. § 391 et. seq.; Driver Qualification File Checklist, Trucking Checklists 2.
[162] For example, See Transportation Rules of the Georgia Public Service Commission 4-1-391 et. seq.
[163] 49 C.F.R. § 391.21; Driver Application Checklist, Trucking Checklists 1.

--- 38 ---

moving violations report ("MVR") from any state issuing a license to the driver for the preceding three-year period.[164] Federal regulations specifically require motor carriers to obtain from prior employers: (1) employment verification, (2) a list of any accidents, and (3) violations of alcohol or controlled substances regulations and test results.[165] The prior employers are required to provide this information to the prospective employer.[166] The motor carrier must verify that the driver is physically able to operate a commercial vehicle by obtaining a medical examiner's certificate to this effect.[167]

The company must either give the driver a road test to determine his ability to operate a commercial vehicle or confirm that he has a commercial driver's license ("CDL") issued from a jurisdiction that requires the driver to pass a road test as part of its licensing procedure.[168]

---

[164] 49 C.F.R. § 391.23.
[165] 49 C.F.R. § 391.23.
[166] 49 C.F.R. § 391.23(g).
[167] 49 C.F.R. § 391.41 & 391.43.
[168] 49 C.F.R. § 391.31 & 391.33.

Road Test

DRIVER'S ROAD TEST EXAMINATION

Driver's Name _____ Phone _____

Driver's Address _____

City _____ State _____ Zip Code _____

The road test shall be given by the motor carrier or a person designated by them. However, a driver who is a motor carrier must be given the test by another person. The test shall be given by a person who is competent to evaluate and determine whether the person who takes the test has demonstrated that he or she is capable of operating the vehicle and associated equipment that the motor carrier intends to assign.

Rating of Performance

- **OK**   The pretrip inspection. (As required by Sec. 392.7)
- **N/a**   Coupling and uncoupling of combination units, if the equipment he or she may drive includes combination units.
- **OK**   Placing the equipment in operation.
- **OK**   Use of vehicle's controls and emergency equipment.
- **OK**   Operating the vehicle in traffic and while passing other vehicles.
- **OK**   Turning the vehicle.
- **OK**   Braking, and slowing the vehicle by means other than braking.
- **OK**   Backing and parking the vehicle.
- _____ Other; Explain: _____

Type of equipment used in giving test: **Tractor/Tandem**

Date **8/28/97**   Examiner's Signature _____

If the road test is successfully completed, the person who gave it shall complete a certificate of driver's road test.

Remarks: _____

We have handled cases in the past where a driver failed his road test multiple times but was still hired by the company.

If the driver is given a road test, he must be tested on his skill in (1) performing pre-trip inspections, (2) coupling and uncoupling of units, (3) placing a commercial vehicle in operation, (4) using controls and emergency equipment, (5) operating a commercial vehicle in traffic, (6) turning the vehicle, (7) braking and slowing the vehicle, and (8) backing and parking the vehicle.[169] A company is also required to make sure that the driver is knowledgeable of the proper manner of securing cargo before allowing him to operate a commercial vehicle.[170] These regulations provide only a minimum standard, and a motor carrier can adopt more stringent requirements for its drivers.[171]

**Practice Pointer: Verify that the trucking company actually contacted the driver's prior employers and examine closely any gaps in a driver's employment history.

---

[169] 49 C.F.R. § 391.31(c).
[170] 49 C.F.R. § 391.13.
[171] Cassara v. DAC Services, Inc., 2002 WL 59687 (10th Cir. 2002).

B. Pre-Employment Screening Report

The FMCSA has created a database on truck drivers as part of its Pre-Employment Screening Process ("PSP"). A motor carrier may access a PSP report on a truck driver who has submitted a drivers application. The PSP report contains information on the results of the any audits, inspections or accidents involving the driver. The PSP report cannot be accessed by the public.

Truck Driver PSP Report

The PSP Report is normally kept in the driver's qualification file of the driver.

C. Federal Minimum Standards for Driver Qualifications

The federal regulations provide a minimum standard for determining the qualifications of a driver.[172] According to these regulations, a driver is qualified to operate a commercial vehicle if he (1) is at least 21 years old; (2) can read and understand the English language sufficient to complete necessary reports, converse with the public and understand traffic signs; (3) can by reason of experience and/or training operate safely a commercial vehicle; (4) is physically qualified to operate a commercial vehicle; (5) has a valid CDL; (6) has completed the driver's application for employment and has provided the company with the required list of prior moving violations and accidents; (7) is not disqualified under any federal regulation; and (8) has successfully completed a road test or has a CDL from a jurisdiction that requires the driver to pass a road test as part of its licensing procedure.[173]

In addition to these specific qualifications, commercial drivers are also required to have the requisite skill and knowledge to operate a commercial vehicle safely.[174] Drivers must have knowledge of (1) safety regulations, (2) commercial motor vehicle safety control systems, (3) safe vehicle operations and control, (4) the relationship of cargo to vehicle control, (5) vehicle inspection procedures, (6) minimal hazardous materials knowledge, and (7) air brake operations and control.[175] A driver must

---

[172] 49 C.F.R. § 391.1.
[173] 49 C.F.R. § 391.11.
[174] 49 C.F.R. § 383.110.
[175] 49 C.F.R. § 383.111.

be familiar with the proper manner of securing cargo and be able to secure properly any cargo transported by him.[176]

D. Entry Level Drivers

An entry level driver is a driver with a CDL with less than one year of experience operating a commercial motor vehicle in interstate commerce.[177] Entry level drivers must receive training from the motor carrier on (1) driver qualifications, (2) hours of service, (3) driver wellness, and (4) whistleblower protection.[178] A carrier must ensure that each entry level driver has a training certificate as proof that he received his entry level training.[179] A copy of the driver's training certificate must be kept in the driver's qualification file.[180] The regulations governing entry level drivers have been held to be constitutional although critics claim that the rules do not contain enough substantive training requirements.[181]

E. Driver Disqualification

Commercial drivers are disqualified for various lengths of time for serious traffic violations.[182] Under this comprehensive scheme, drivers are disqualified from operating a commercial vehicle for 60 days for any second conviction within a three year period of any combination of any offense committed in a commercial vehicle of (1) speeding in excess of 15 mph over the speed limit, (2) driving recklessly, (3) making improper or erratic lane changes, (4) following the vehicle ahead too closely, (5) violating any motor vehicle traffic control law arising in connection with a fatal accident, (6) texting while driving or (7) driving without a commercial driver's license.[183] A driver is disqualified for one year for driving under the influence of alcohol or controlled substances or leaving the scene of an accident, whether the offense occurs in a commercial vehicle or a non-commercial vehicle, and for causing a fatality as a result of the negligent operation of a commercial vehicle.[184] A driver is also disqualified for a year if he continues to operate a commercial vehicle after having been disqualified.[185] Drivers are also subject to disqualification for in excess of 60 days for violations of railroad crossing regulations and for violations of out-of-service orders.[186] The penalties increase for multiple offenses or repeat violations of the same offense.[187] A motor carrier has an obligation to make sure that a disqualified driver does not operate a commercial vehicle.[188]

Practice Pointer: Request copies of any records of disqualifications or out-of-service citations concerning the driver.

F. Commercial Learner's Permit

A person may obtain a Commercial Learner's Permit (CLP) by taking the written exam required of a CDL driver without completing the skills test.[189] The holder of a CLP can operate a commercial vehicle on the roadway as long as he has a valid regular drivers license and is accompanied by a driver who has a current CDL license.[190]

---

[176] 49 C.F.R. § 391.13.
[177] 49 C.F.R. § 380.502.
[178] 49 C.F.R. § 380.503.
[179] 49 C.F.R. § 380.505.
[180] 49 C.F.R. § 380.509.
[181] Advocates for Highway & Auto Safety v. FMCSA, 429 F.3d 1136 (D.C. 2005).
[182] 49 C.F.R. § 383.51.
[183] 49 C.F.R. § 383.51.
[184] 49 C.F.R. § 383.51.
[185] 49 C.F.R. § 383.51.
[186] 49 C.F.R. § 383.51.
[187] 49 C.F.R. § 383.51.
[188] 49 C.F.R. § 383.51(a).
[189] 49 C.F.R. § 383.71.
[190] 49 C.F.R. § 383.71.

G. Commercial Driver's Licenses

A driver may not operate a commercial vehicle on his own unless the driver has obtained a valid commercial driver's license ("CDL").[191] A driver may have only one CDL at any time.[192] CDLs are divided into three separate motor vehicle groups. Group A is for the operation of any combination of vehicles with a gross vehicle weight rating ("GVWR") in excess of 26,000 lbs. provided the GVWR of the vehicle(s) being towed is in excess of 10,000 lbs.[193] Group B is for the operation of any single vehicle with a GVWR in excess of 26,000 lbs. or any vehicle towing a vehicle not in excess of 10,000 lbs.[194] Group C is for the operation of any vehicles not covered in Group A or B which is designed to transport 16 or more passengers or is used in transporting hazardous materials.[195] The requirement for a CDL may be waived by State law in regards to farmers, firefighters, emergency response vehicles, drivers removing ice and snow and the fireworks industry.[196]

**Practice Pointer: Make sure the driver is not hiding prior violations by maintaining more than one CDL.

H. Endorsements to CDL

Special endorsements to a CDL are required in order for a driver to operate certain commercial vehicles such as double/triple trailers, passenger vehicles, tankers or vehicles transporting hazardous materials.[197] A driver must demonstrate special knowledge about coupling and uncoupling double/triple trailers to obtain a double/triple trailer endorsement.[198] In order to have a passenger endorsement, a driver must have knowledge about proper procedures for unloading/loading passengers, use of emergency exits, proper responses to emergency situations such as fires or unruly passengers, proper procedures at railroad crossings and drawbridges, and appropriate braking procedures.[199] A driver with a tank vehicle endorsement must understand (1) causes, prevention and effects of cargo surge on motor vehicle handling, (2) proper braking procedures when the tank is empty, full and partially full, (3) differences in handling baffled/ compartmental tank interiors versus non-baffled ones, (4) differences in cargo surge for each kind of liquid, (5) effects of road grade and curvature on motor vehicle handling, (6) proper use of emergency systems, and (7) retest and marking requirements.[200] In order to obtain a hazardous materials endorsement, a driver must demonstrate that he has knowledge of hazardous materials regulations, hazardous materials handling, operation of safety equipment, and emergency response procedures.[201] School bus drivers must demonstrate the ability to deal with passengers and skills in loading and unloading children to obtain an endorsement.[202]

I. Physical Requirements

A driver is not physically qualified to operate a motor vehicle if he (1) has lost a foot, leg, hand or arm or has an impairment of his foot, leg, hand or arm which interferes with his ability to drive; (2) has diabetes mellitus requiring insulin for control; (3) has a serious heart condition; (4) has a history of respiratory dysfunction; (5) has high blood pressure or joint or muscular problems which interfere with his ability to drive; (6) has epilepsy or any other condition which might cause a loss of consciousness; (7) has a mental or psychiatric disorder which interferes with his ability to drive; (8) has less than 20/40 vision with corrective lenses; (9) has significant hearing loss; (10) takes a

---

[191] 49 U.S.C. § 31302.
[192] 49 U.S.C. § 31302; 49 C.F.R. § 383.21.
[193] 49 C.F.R. § 383.91(a).
[194] 49 C.F.R. § 383.91(a).
[195] 49 C.F.R. § 383.91(a).
[196] 49 C.F.R. § 383.3.
[197] 49 C.F.R. § 383.93.
[198] 49 C.F.R. § 383.115.
[199] 49 C.F.R. § 383.117.
[200] 49 C.F.R. § 383.119.
[201] 49 C.F.R. § 383.121.
[202] 49 C.F.R. § 383.123.

controlled substance which interferes with the ability to drive; or (11) has a clinical diagnosis of alcoholism.[203] As part of SAFETEA-LU, the FMCSA must grant an exemption to insulin dependent diabetics who have demonstrated that they have control over their diabetes for at least 2 months if Type I diabetes and at least 1 month if Type II Diabetes until the regulations are amended to remove the disqualification for insulin dependent diabetes.[204] A trucking company can be held responsible for allowing a driver with a medical condition that leads to sleepiness or fatigue to operate a commercial vehicle resulting in an accident.[205]

The driver's physical exam must be repeated every two years or whenever a physical or mental injury or disease impairs his ability to perform his normal duties.[206] The medical exam must be performed by a certified medical examiner listed on the National Registry of Certified Medical Examiners.[207]

Medical Card

An accident can be the result of a driver having a medical condition such as sleep apnea, seizures or diabetes.

If a driver is determined by a medical examiner not to be qualified to drive and the driver locates another physician to dispute the finding, the driver may apply to the Director of Office of Motor Carrier Research and Standards to resolve the conflict in medical evaluations.[208] A driver may also apply for a waiver of certain physical defects which would otherwise result in disqualification.[209]

Practice Pointer: Request copies of the driver's medical records to determine his physical qualifications.

---

[203] 49 C.F.R. § 391.41.
[204] Pub. L. 109-59, August 10, 2005, 119 Stat. 1144.
[205] Lewis v. D. Hays Trucking, Inc., 701 F.Supp.2d 1300 (N.D.Ga. 2010).
[206] 49 C.F.R. § 391.45.
[207] 49 C.F.R. § 391.43.
[208] 49 C.F.R. § 391.47.
[209] 49 C.F.R. § 391.49.

J. Annual Review of Driving Record

During the course of a driver's employment, the trucking company must perform an annual review of the driver at least every twelve months to determine if the driver is still qualified to operate a commercial vehicle.[210]

Annual Review

MOTOR VEHICLE DRIVER'S CERTIFICATION & ANNUAL REVIEW OF DRIVING RECORD

I certify that the following is a true and complete list of traffic violations (other than parking violations) for which I have been convicted or forfeited bond or collateral during the past 12 months.

DATE	OFFENSE	LOCATION	TYPE OF VEHICLE OPERATED
	N/A		
	N/A		
	N/A		
	N/A		

If no violations are listed above, I certify that I have not been convicted or forfeited bond or collateral on any violations required to be listed during the past 12 months.

_____ Date   _____ Driver's Signature

_____ Motor Carrier's Name   _____ Motor Carrier's Address

_____ Reviewed by - Signature   Safety Title

In accordance with Section 391.25 of the FMCSR I have carefully reviewed the driving record of the driver shown above to determine whether or not he / she meets the minimum requirements for safe driving specified in Section 391.11 of title 49 Code of Federal Regulations or is disqualified to drive a motor vehicle pursuant to Section 391.15.

In reviewing this driver's record, I have considered any evidence that the driver has violated applicable provisions of the FMCSR and the Hazardous Materials Regulations. I have also considered the driver's accident record and any evidence that the driver has violated laws governing the operation of a motor vehicle, and gave great weight to violations, such as speeding, reckless driving and operating while under the influence of alcohol or drugs, that indicate that the driver has exhibited a disregard for the safety of the public.

This driver is (✓) QUALIFIED ( ) DISQUALIFIED to operate a commercial motor vehicle.

COMMENTS/REMARKS_____

3-6-98 Date   _____ Signature   Safety Title

The company must continually monitor the performance of the driver in order to avoid a negligent retention claim.

In conjunction with this review, the driver must provide a certified list of all moving violations and accidents for the preceding twelve-month period.[211] The company is required to run an MVR on the driver to verify this information.[212] The company must then consider the driver's accident record and driving history in deciding if the driver is still qualified to operate a commercial vehicle.[213] The trucking company must give great weight to violations that indicate that the driver has exhibited a disregard for the safety of the public, such as speeding, reckless driving, or operating a vehicle while under the influence of alcohol or drugs.[214]

**Practice Pointer: Make sure the trucking company conducted an annual review of the driver and actually considered whether he was qualified to continue operating a vehicle.

---

[210] 49 C.F.R. § 391.25.
[211] 49 C.F.R. § 391.27.
[212] 49 C.F.R. § 391.25.
[213] 49 C.F.R. § 391.25(b)(2).
[214] 49 C.F.R. § 391.25(b)(2).

K. Maintenance of Driver's Qualification File

The trucking company is required to maintain a driver's qualification file on each driver.[215] The driver's qualification file must contain: (1) the driver's application for employment; (2) a written record of inquiries to prior employers and any responses received from them; (3) the pre-employment MVR on the driver; (4) results of any road test or a copy of the driver's CDL; (5) the driver's annual review; (6) the MVR on the driver related to the annual review; (7) the driver's certified list of moving violations and accidents provided in conjunction with the annual review; and (8) the medical examiner's certificate of physical qualification.[216] The documents in the driver's qualification file must be kept by the company for as long as the driver is employed by the company and for an additional three-year period, except that documents related to the annual review may be discarded following a subsequent annual review and the medical examiner's certificate may be discarded every two years following the replacement with a new certificate.[217] A motor carrier does not have to maintain a driver's qualification file on any driver who is not regularly employed by the carrier if the driver is employed regularly by another carrier and the other carrier certifies in writing that the driver is fully qualified to operate a commercial vehicle.[218]

**Practice Pointer: Request the entire driver's qualification file.

L. Driver's Duty to Notify His Employer of Violations

Within one business day after the date of the action, a driver must notify the trucking company if his driver's license is revoked, suspended or canceled, if he loses the right to operate a commercial vehicle for any reason or if he is disqualified from operating a commercial vehicle.[219] A driver must notify the company of any violation of any State or local law concerning motor vehicle traffic control within thirty days after the date the driver is found to have committed the violation.[220] A motor carrier may not allow a driver to operate a commercial vehicle if the driver's license has been revoked, suspended, or canceled or the driver has more than one driver's license.[221] The Surface Transportation Board maintains a database on the licensing, identification and disqualification of commercial drivers.[222]

---

[215] 49 C.F.R. § 391.51(a); Driver Qualification File Checklist, Trucking Checklists 2.
[216] 49 C.F.R. § 391.51(b).
[217] 49 C.F.R. § 391.51(c).
[218] 49 C.F.R. § 391.65.
[219] 49 U.S.C. § 31303(b); 49 C.F.R. § 383.33.
[220] 49 U.S.C. § 31303(a); 49 C.F.R. § 383.31.
[221] 49 U.S.C. § 31304; 49 C.F.R. § 383.37(a)&(b).
[222] 49 U.S.C. § 31309.

IV. The Commercial Driver's License (CDL) Manual

Each state has its own Commercial Driver's License (CDL) Manual that contains similar model language on safe operations of a commercial vehicle. The CDL Manual establishes rules and guidelines that the professional truck driver must be knowledgeable of in order to obtain a CDL and comprises industry standards that must be followed by drivers and trucking companies. A failure to follow the provisions of the CDL Manual is evidence of negligence on the part of the driver and/or trucking company.[223]

In Section 2.1, the CDL Manual gives detailed instructions on how to perform a pre-trip inspection on a tractor and trailer.[224] A truck driver should know the parts to be examined in conducting a pre-trip inspection and the steps necessary to complete an appropriate inspection. In any improper repair and maintenance or mechanical failure case, this section from the CDL Manual should be fully explored with the driver and corporate representative of the trucking company.

A. Backing a Tractor Trailer

The CDL Manual has the following explanation and warnings concerning backing a tractor trailer.[225]

> **2.2.4 – Backing Safely**
>
> Because you cannot see everything behind your vehicle, backing is always dangerous. Avoid backing whenever you can. When you park, try to park so you will be able to pull forward when you leave. When you have to back, here are a few simple safety rules:
>
> Start in the proper position.
> Look at your path.
> Use mirrors on both sides.
> Back slowly.
> Back and turn toward the driver's side whenever possible.
> Use a helper whenever possible.

---

[223] Rabon v. Hopkins, 703 S.E.2d 181 (N.C. 2010); Schultz v. Lester, 2011 WL 3211271 (Tx. 2011); Langille v. Transco, Inc., 2013 WL 6185347 (D.Wy. 2013).
[224] CDL Manual Section 2.1.
[225] CDL Manual Section 2.2.4.

B. Failure to Maintain a Proper Lookout

The CDL Manual establishes that a truck driver should be looking 12 to 15 seconds ahead of him to make sure there are no hazards in the roadway.[226]

2.4.1 – Seeing Ahead

All drivers look ahead; but many don't look far enough ahead.

Importance of Looking Far Enough Ahead. Because stopping or changing lanes can take a lot of distance, knowing what the traffic is doing on all sides of you is very important. You need to look well ahead to make sure you have room to make these moves safely.

How Far Ahead to Look. Most good drivers look at least 12 to 15 seconds ahead. That means looking ahead the distance you will travel in 12 to 15 seconds. At lower speeds, that's about one block. At highway speeds it's about a quarter of a mile. If you're not looking that far ahead, you may have to stop too quickly or make quick lane changes. Looking 12 to 15 seconds ahead doesn't mean not paying attention to things that are closer. Good drivers shift their attention back and forth, near and far. Figure 2.6 illustrates how far to look ahead.

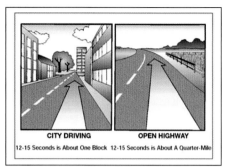

Figure 2.6

Look for Traffic. Look for vehicles coming onto the highway, into your lane, or turning. Watch for brake lights from slowing vehicles. By seeing these things far enough ahead, you can change your speed, or change lanes if necessary to avoid a problem. If a traffic light has been green for a long time it will probably change before you get there. Start slowing down and be ready to stop.

---

[226] CDL Manual Section 2.4.1.

C. Following Too Closely

A truck driver must maintain 6 seconds of distance between himself and the vehicle in front of him at speeds of 55 mph.[227]

How Much Space? How much space should you keep in front of you? One good rule says you need at least one second for each 10 feet of vehicle length at speeds below 40 mph. At greater speeds, you must add 1 second for safety. For example, if you are driving a 40-foot vehicle, you should leave 4 seconds between you and the vehicle ahead. In a 60-foot rig, you'll need 6 seconds. Over 40 mph, you'd need 5 seconds for a 40-foot vehicle and 7 seconds for a 60-foot vehicle. See Figure 2.12.

To know how much space you have, wait until the vehicle ahead passes a shadow on the road, a pavement marking, or some other clear landmark. Then count off the seconds like this: "one thousand- and-one, one thousand-and-two" and so on, until you reach the same spot. Compare your count with the rule of one second for every ten feet of length.

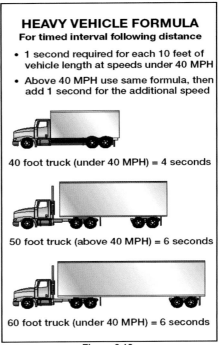

HEAVY VEHICLE FORMULA
For timed interval following distance
- 1 second required for each 10 feet of vehicle length at speeds under 40 MPH
- Above 40 MPH use same formula, then add 1 second for the additional speed

40 foot truck (under 40 MPH) = 4 seconds

50 foot truck (above 40 MPH) = 6 seconds

60 foot truck (under 40 MPH) = 6 seconds

Figure 2.12

If you are driving a 40-foot truck and only counted up to 2 seconds, you're too close. Drop back a little and count again until you have 4 seconds of following distance (or 5 seconds, if you're going over 40 mph). After a little practice, you will know how far back you should be. Remember to add 1 second for speeds above 40 mph. Also remember that when the road is slippery, you need much more space to stop.

D. Lane Changes

The CDL Manual describes the appropriate manner for a truck driver to make a lane change to make sure he identifies if there are any vehicles in his blind spot.[228]

Lane Changes. You need to check your mirrors to make sure no one is alongside you or about to pass you. Check your mirrors:

Before you change lanes to make sure there is enough room.
After you have signaled, to check that no one has moved into your blind spot.
Right after you start the lane change, to double-check that your path is clear.
After you complete the lane change.

---

[227] CDL Manual Section 2.7.1.
[228] CDL Manual Section 2.4.2.

E. Crossing Traffic

A truck driver cannot attempt to cross lanes of traffic unless he is sure he can make it to the other side before traffic reaches his tractor-trailer.[229]

> **2.7.7 – Space Needed to Cross or Enter Traffic**
>
> Be aware of the size and weight of your vehicle when you cross or enter traffic. Here are some important things to keep in mind.
>
> Because of slow acceleration and the space large vehicles require, you may need a much larger gap to enter traffic than you would in a car.
> Acceleration varies with the load. Allow more room if your vehicle is heavily loaded.
> Before you start across a road, make sure you can get all the way across before traffic reaches you.

---

[229] CDL Manual Section 2.7.7.

F. Stopping on the Side of the Roadway

It is important for the truck driver to use his hazard lights and place warning signals behind his vehicle whenever he is stopped on the side of the roadway.[230]

When Parked at the Side of the Road. When you pull off the road and stop, be sure to turn on the four-way emergency flashers. This is important at night. Don't trust the taillights to give warning. Drivers have crashed into the rear of a parked vehicle because they thought it was moving normally.

If you must stop on a road or the shoulder of any road, you must put out your emergency warning devices within ten minutes. Place your warning devices at the following locations:

If you must stop on or by a one-way or divided highway, place warning devices 10 feet, 100 feet, and 200 feet toward the approaching traffic. See Figure 2.8.

If you stop on a two-lane road carrying traffic in both directions or on an undivided highway, place warning devices within 10 feet of the front or rear corners to mark the location of the vehicle and 100 feet behind and ahead of the vehicle, on the shoulder or in the lane you stopped in. See Figure 2.9.

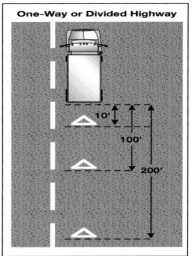

Figure 2.8

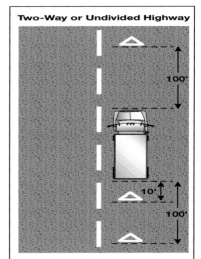

Figure 2.9

Back beyond any hill, curve, or other obstruction that prevents other drivers from seeing the vehicle within 500 feet. If line of sight view is obstructed due to hill or curve, move the rear-most triangle to a point back down the road so warning is provided.

---

[230] CDL Manual Section 2.5.2.

G. Stopping Distances

Truck drivers should know that it takes 450 feet to stop at 55 mph and be able to calculate stopping distances at different speeds.[231]

2.6.1 – Stopping Distance

Perception Distance + Reaction Distance + Braking Distance =Total Stopping Distance

Perception Distance. This is the distance your vehicle travels from the time your eyes see a hazard until your brain recognizes it. The perception time for an alert driver is about 3/4 second. At 55 mph, you travel 60 feet in 3/4 second or about 81 feet per second.

Reaction Distance. The distance traveled from the time your brain tells your foot to move from the accelerator until your foot is actually pushing the brake pedal. The average driver has a reaction time of 3/4 second. This accounts for an additional 60 feet traveled at 55 mph.

Braking Distance. The distance it takes to stop once the brakes are put on. At 55 mph on dry pavement with good brakes, it can take a heavy vehicle about 390 feet to stop. It takes about 4 1/2 seconds.

Total Stopping Distance. At 55 mph, it will take about six seconds to stop and your vehicle will travel about 450 feet.

The Effect of Speed on Stopping Distance. The faster you drive, the greater the impact or striking power of your vehicle. When you double your speed from 20 to 40 mph the impact is 4 times greater. The braking distance is also 4 times longer. Triple the speed from 20 to 60 mph and the impact and braking distance is 9 times greater. At 60 mph, your stopping distance is greater than that of a football field. Increase the speed to 80 mph and the impact and braking distance are 16 times greater than at 20 mph. High speeds greatly increase the severity of crashes and stopping distances. By slowing down, you can reduce braking distance. See Figure 2.11

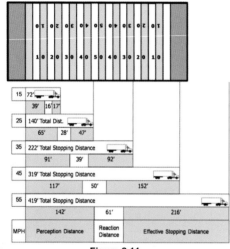

Figure 2.11

H. Nighttime Driving

A truck driver must be able to stop within the distance he can see ahead of him.[232]

2.6.4 – Speed and Distance Ahead

You should always be able to stop within the distance you can see ahead. Fog, rain, or other conditions may require that you slow down to be able to stop in the distance you can see. At night, you can't see as far with low beams as you can with high beams. When you must use low beams, slow down.

---

[231] CDL Manual Section 2.6.1.
[232] CDL Manual Section 2.6.4.

With his low beams on, a truck driver can see 250 feet in front of him and can see 350 to 500 feet in front of him with high beams activated.[233]

> **Headlights.** At night your headlights will usually be the main source of light for you to see by and for others to see you. You can't see nearly as much with your headlights as you see in the daytime. With low beams you can see ahead about 250 feet and with high beams about 350-500 feet. You must adjust your speed to keep your stopping distance within your sight distance. This means going slowly enough to be able to stop within the range of your headlights. Otherwise, by the time you see a hazard, you will not have time to stop.

Given that it takes 450 feet to stop at 55 mph, a truck driver must have his high beams on to drive 55 mph at night in order to be able to stop within the visibility of his headlights.[234] A truck driver is overdriving his headlights and violating industry standards if he is driving with his low beams on at 55 mph. The truck driver's failure to drive with high beams activated at night is a common cause of nighttime accidents.[235]

> **Use High Beams When You Can.** Some drivers make the mistake of always using low beams. This seriously cuts down on their ability to see ahead. Use high beams when it is safe and legal to do so. Use them when you are not within 500 feet of an approaching vehicle. Also, don't let the inside of your cab get too bright. This makes it harder to see outside. Keep the interior light off, and adjust your instrument lights as low as you can to still be able to read the gauges.

I. Driving in the Rain

Truck drivers should reduce their speed by one-third, i.e. from 55 mph to 35 mph, when the roads are wet.[236]

> **Slippery Surfaces.** It will take longer to stop, and it will be harder to turn without skidding, when the road is slippery. Wet roads can double stopping distance. You must drive slower to be able to stop in the same distance as on a dry road. Reduce speed by about one-third (e.g., slow from 55 to about 35 mph) on a wet road. On packed snow, reduce speed by a half, or more. If the surface is icy, reduce speed to a crawl and stop driving as soon as you can safely do so.

---

[233] CDL Manual Section 2.11.4.
[234] CDL Manual Section 2.6.1.
[235] CDL Manual Section 2.11.5.
[236] CDL Manual Section 2.6.2.

J. Driving in Fog

The CDL Manual warns truck drivers to avoid driving in fog.[237]

> **2.12 – Driving in Fog**
>
> Fog can occur at any time. Fog on highways can be extremely dangerous. Fog is often unexpected, and visibility can deteriorate rapidly. You should watch for foggy conditions and be ready to reduce your speed. Do not assume that the fog will thin out after you enter it.
>
> The best advice for driving in fog is don't. It is preferable that you pull off the road into a rest area or truck stop until visibility is better. If you must drive, be sure to consider the following:
>
> Obey all fog-related warning signs.
> Slow down before you enter fog.
> Use low-beam headlights and fog lights for best visibility even in daytime, and be alert for other drivers who may have forgotten to turn on their lights.
> Turn on your 4-way flashers. This will give vehicles approaching you from behind a quicker opportunity to notice your vehicle.
> Watch for vehicles on the side of the roadway. Seeing taillights or headlights in front of you may not be a true indication of where the road is ahead of you. The vehicle may not be on the road at all.
> Use roadside highway reflectors as guides to determine how the road may curve ahead of you.
> Listen for traffic you cannot see.
> Avoid passing other vehicles.
> Don't stop along the side of the road, unless absolutely necessary.

**Practice Pointer: Use the CDL Manual to establish industry standards and to show that the truck driver intentionally broke the rules of safe operations thereby placing the public at risk.

---

[237] CDL Manual Section 2.12.

V. Alcohol and Controlled Substance Testing

Federal regulations establish strict guidelines for alcohol and controlled substance use by drivers and testing by carriers.[238] These guidelines apply to every person who operates a commercial motor vehicle in commerce in any state if he is subject to the commercial driver's license requirements in the United States, Mexico or Canada.[239] Federal law preempts state law in regards to drug and alcohol testing of drivers to the extent that compliance with both the state and federal requirements is not possible or compliance with the state law is an obstacle to the accomplishment and execution of the federal law.[240] Pursuant to this preemption provision, state and local governments may not attempt to regulate the time and manner of a motor carrier's drug testing program.[241]

A. Use of Alcohol While On Duty

A driver cannot use alcohol within 4 hours of going on duty or being physically in control of or operating a commercial vehicle.[242] A driver may not possess wine, beer or distilled spirits while on duty or operating a commercial vehicle.[243] A motor carrier cannot permit a driver to operate a commercial vehicle if it appears by his conduct or appearance that he has consumed alcohol within 4 hours.[244] Any driver who appears to have consumed alcohol within 4 hours of going on duty or operating a commercial vehicle must be placed out-of-service for a 24-hour period.[245]

A driver also cannot use alcohol while performing a safety sensitive function[246] and cannot report for duty or remain on duty requiring the performance of a safety-sensitive function while having an alcohol concentration of 0.04 or greater.[247] A safety-sensitive function includes operating a commercial vehicle, being present in a commercial vehicle except time spent resting in a sleeper berth, waiting at a terminal, facility or other property for dispatch unless the driver has been relieved by his employer, inspecting, servicing or conditioning a commercial vehicle, loading or unloading a vehicle or assisting in the loading or unloading process, or repairing or attending to a disabled vehicle.[248] A trucking company is prohibited from allowing a driver who has used alcohol within 4 hours,[249] is using alcohol,[250] or has an alcohol concentration of 0.04 or greater[251] to perform or continue to perform a safety sensitive function. A driver who is found to have an alcohol concentration of greater than 0.02 but less than 0.04 cannot perform or continue to perform safety-sensitive functions until at least 24 hours after the alcohol test.[252] A jury issue exists as to whether an intoxicated driver acts outside the scope of his employment with the trucking company when the company's policies forbid alcohol use.[253]

Practice Pointer: Request copies of all alcohol tests performed on the driver and correspondence with prior employers about alcohol use.

---

[238] 49 C.F.R. § 382 et. seq.
[239] 49 C.F.R. § 382.103(a).
[240] 49 C.F.R. § 382.109(a).
[241] Visnovec v. Yellow Freight System, Inc., 754 F.Supp. 142 (D.Minn. 1990); Yellow Freight System, Inc. v. Amestoy, 736 F.Supp. 44 (D.Vermont 1990).
[242] 49 C.F.R. § 392.5(a)(1).
[243] 49 C.F.R. § 392.5(a).
[244] 49 C.F.R. § 392.5(b).
[245] 49 C.F.R. § 392.5(c).
[246] 49 C.F.R. § 382.205.
[247] 49 C.F.R. § 382.201.
[248] 49 C.F.R. § 382.107.
[249] 49 C.F.R. § 382.207.
[250] 49 C.F.R. § 382.205.
[251] 49 C.F.R. § 382.201.
[252] 49 C.F.R. § 382.505(a).
[253] Minter v. Great American Insurance Co. of NY, 423 F.3d 460 (5th Cir. 2005).

B. Use of Controlled Substances While On Duty

A driver cannot use a controlled substance when reporting for or remaining on duty requiring the performance of a safety-sensitive function unless the use of the controlled substance is pursuant to the instructions of a physician who has advised the driver that the substance will not adversely affect his ability to safely operate a commercial vehicle.[254] A motor carrier may require a driver to disclose any therapeutic drug use related to a medical condition.[255] A driver cannot report for duty, remain on duty or perform a safety sensitive function if he tests positive for controlled substances.[256] An employer is prohibited from allowing a driver who has used controlled substances[257] or tests positive for a controlled substance[258] to perform or continue to perform a safety sensitive function.

Practice Pointer: Request copies of all controlled substances tests performed on the driver and correspondence with prior employers about drug use.

C. Pre-Employment Alcohol & Drug Screening

A trucking company must provide its drivers with educational material explaining its policies and procedures and federal guidelines concerning alcohol and controlled substance testing prior to conducting a pre-employment alcohol and controlled substances screen.[259] A motor carrier must complete a pre-employment screen of a driver for alcohol and controlled substances before the driver performs his first safety-sensitive function for the carrier.[260] A carrier may not allow a driver to perform a safety-sensitive function until the driver has undergone an alcohol test with a result indicating an alcohol concentration less than 0.04 and has undergone a controlled substances test with a negative result.[261] A carrier does not have to perform a pre-employment alcohol test if the driver has been tested in the last six months with a result of less than 0.04, and the carrier ensures that the driver's prior employer has no record of a violation of the alcohol use prohibition within the last six months.[262]

A pre-employment controlled substance test is not necessary if the driver was tested for controlled substances within the past six months or was involved in a random testing program for the past twelve months AND the carrier contacts the driver's prior employer to ensure that the driver did not violate any prohibitions within the past six months.[263] A carrier who does not conduct a pre-employment screen under the aforementioned exceptions must obtain a copy of the driver's alcohol and/or drug testing records from his prior testing program.[264] A carrier who does not employ a driver but uses him more than once a year must obtain the driver's alcohol and controlled substance testing records from his primary employer every six months or must conduct its own testing of the driver.[265]

A carrier must also request all alcohol test results greater than 0.04, all positive controlled substances results, and all refusals to be tested from a driver's prior employers for the two-year period preceding the application for employment.[266] This information must be reviewed by a carrier no later than 14 days after the first time a driver performs a safety-sensitive function.[267] If a carrier cannot obtain these records after making a good faith effort, the carrier must document in the driver's qualification file

---

[254] 49 C.F.R. § 382.213(a).
[255] 49 C.F.R. § 382.213(c).
[256] 49 C.F.R. § 382.215.
[257] 49 C.F.R. § 382.213(b).
[258] 49 C.F.R. § 382.215.
[259] 49 C.F.R. § 382.601(a).
[260] 49 C.F.R. § 382.301(a).
[261] 49 C.F.R. § 382.301(a).
[262] 49 C.F.R. § 382.301(b).
[263] 49 C.F.R. § 382.301(c).
[264] 49 C.F.R. § 382.301(d)(1).
[265] 49 C.F.R. § 382.301(d)(2).
[266] 49 C.F.R. § 382.413(a)(1).
[267] 49 C.F.R. § 382.413(b).

the efforts made to obtain the records.[268] A carrier who obtains information that a driver has violated the alcohol or controlled substances requirements may not employ the driver until the carrier has obtained information on subsequent compliance with the referral and rehabilitation requirements.[269]

**Practice Pointer: Request all pre-employment drug and alcohol screens and any information provided to drivers about drug and alcohol testing.

D. Reasonable Suspicion Testing

If a motor carrier has a reasonable suspicion that a driver has violated the alcohol use prohibitions, the carrier must require the driver to submit to testing.[270] This reasonable suspicion must be based on the appearance, behavior, speech or body odor of the driver.[271] A supervisor or company official who has received specific training regarding the use of alcohol shall make the determination that a reasonable suspicion to conduct testing exists.[272] Carriers are required to provide these supervisors with at least one hour of alcohol misuse training and one hour of controlled substances training in order to identify violators.[273] The supervisor must witness the alleged violation during, just preceding or just after the period of the workday.[274] The supervisor making the determination is prohibited from conducting the alcohol test on the driver.[275] If the alcohol test is not performed within two hours of the determination of a reasonable suspicion, the carrier must prepare and maintain a record stating the reasons the test was not completed in a timely fashion.[276] If the carrier fails to conduct a test within eight hours, the carrier shall cease any attempts to complete the test.[277] After a determination that a reasonable suspicion exists for a violation, a carrier may not allow a driver to report for duty or remain on duty requiring the performance of safety-sensitive functions until an alcohol test is completed with a result of less than 0.02 blood alcohol concentration, or twenty-four hours has elapsed since the alleged violation.[278]

A carrier must also conduct a controlled substance test if the carrier has a reasonable suspicion that a driver has used a controlled substance.[279] The carrier's reasonable suspicion must be based on the behavior, speech and body odor of the driver especially any indications of chronic or withdrawal effects of controlled substance use.[280] A supervisor or company official who has received specific training regarding the use of controlled substances shall make the determination that a reasonable suspicion to conduct testing exists.[281] The supervisor must make a written record of the observations leading to the controlled substance testing within twenty-four hours of the occurrence or before the results of the test are released, whichever is earlier.[282]

**Practice Pointer: If drug or alcohol use by a driver is an issue, make sure that a supervisor had training in reasonable suspicion testing to detect the driver's use before it became a problem.

---

[268] 49 C.F.R. § 382.413(c).
[269] 49 C.F.R. § 382.413(g).
[270] 49 C.F.R. § 382.307(a).
[271] 49 C.F.R. § 382.307.
[272] 49 C.F.R. § 382.307(c).
[273] 49 C.F.R. § 382.603.
[274] 49 C.F.R. § 382.307(d).
[275] 49 C.F.R. § 382.307(c).
[276] 49 C.F.R. § 382.307(e)(1).
[277] 49 C.F.R. § 382.307(e)(1).
[278] 49 C.F.R. § 382.307(e)(4).
[279] 49 C.F.R. § 382.307(b).
[280] 49 C.F.R. § 382.307(b).
[281] 49 C.F.R. § 382.307(c).
[282] 49 C.F.R. § 382.307(f).

E. Random Drug & Alcohol Testing

A carrier must also conduct random alcohol and drug testing on a certain percentage of its drivers per year regardless of their conduct.[283] The testing must be unannounced and the dates for administering the tests must be spread reasonably throughout the calendar year.[284]

F. Post-Accident Testing

A trucking company must perform a drug and alcohol test on a driver whenever he is involved in an automobile accident resulting in a fatality.[285] Testing is also required when the investigating officer issues a citation to the driver involved in the accident and the accident causes bodily injury requiring immediate treatment away from the accident scene or the accident causes disabling damage to any motor vehicle which must be towed from the scene.[286] Disabling damage does not include damage which can be remedied at the scene without special tools or parts, tire damage without any other damage, headlight or taillight damage, or damage to turn signals, horn or windshield wipers.[287] The post-accident testing should occur as soon as practicable after the accident.[288] A motor carrier's cancellation of a scheduled post-accident test is admissible as evidence tending to show that the carrier was trying to conceal the driver's potential use of alcohol or controlled substances.[289]

If the alcohol test cannot be administered within two hours of the accident, the carrier must maintain on file a record indicating the reason the test was not promptly administered.[290] If the alcohol test cannot be completed within eight hours, the carrier shall cease attempts to conduct the test.[291] The controlled substance test must be performed within 32 hours following an accident, and if not completed within this time frame, the carrier shall cease attempts to conduct the test and shall maintain a record stating the reasons the test was not promptly administered.[292] A carrier does not have to conduct an alcohol or controlled substance test if Federal, State or local officials have already conducted a breath or blood test for alcohol and a urine test for controlled substances.[293] A carrier must provide a driver with the necessary information to complete the post-accident testing, and a driver must take all reasonable steps to comply with the testing procedures.[294] The requirement for post-accident testing does not apply to an occurrence involving boarding or exiting a stationary vehicle, the unloading or loading of cargo, or the operation of a passenger vehicle not for hire.[295] A driver may not use alcohol for eight hours after an accident if he is required to take a post-accident alcohol test.[296]

Practice Pointer: Request all post-accident drug and alcohol test results and notations about the failure to perform post-accident testing. A court order is necessary to obtain the results.

G. Chain of Custody for a Post-Accident Drug Test

When a urine sample is taken from a truck driver, there are two paperwork forms that are completed. One form is sent with the sample to the laboratory with the specimen. This form does not include the driver's name but has a bar code number and the driver's social security number.

---

[283] 49 C.F.R. § 382.305.
[284] 49 C.F.R. § 382.305(k).
[285] 49 C.F.R. § 382.303(a)(1).
[286] 49 C.F.R. § 382.303(a)(2).
[287] 49 C.F.R. § 382.107.
[288] 49 C.F.R. § 382.303(a).
[289] Wanke v. Lynn's Transportation Co., 836 F.Supp. 587 (N.D. Ind. 1993).
[290] 49 C.F.R. § 382.303(b).
[291] 49 C.F.R. § 382.303(b).
[292] 49 C.F.R. § 382.303(b)(4).
[293] 49 C.F.R. § 382.303(e).
[294] 49 C.F.R. § 382.303(c)-(d).
[295] 49 C.F.R. § 382.303(f).
[296] 49 C.F.R. § 382.209.

Laboratory Form Sent with Specimen

SPECIMEN ID NO. 104042528

FEDERAL DRUG TESTING CUSTODY AND CONTROL FORM

DRUGSCAN® Medical and Forensic Toxicology Services P.O. BOX 2969 WARMINSTER, PA. 18974 (215) 674-9310

08071689

STEP 1: COMPLETED BY COLLECTOR OR EMPLOYER REPRESENTATIVE — LAB ACCESSION NO. — MR1001

A. Employer Name, Address, I.D. No. [redacted]
~~J & R SCHUGEL TRUCKING, INC~~
~~ATTN: SAFETY DEPARTMENT~~ PO BOX 1601
~~*Fax:507-354-7463 Ph:507-359-2037*~~
M. Waukee, WI 53201
~~P.O. BOX 278~~ 800-543-9932
~~NEW ULM, MN 56073~~ 414-671-8009
104042528

B. MRO Name, Address, Phone and Fax No.
MAIN LINE MEDICAL REVIEW ASSOCIATES
ATTN: DR. JOSEPH M. DIMINO
Fax:215-443-0670
P.O.BOX 2087, 1117 MEARNS ROAD
WARMINSTER, PA 18974 Ph#: 215-674-3088
~~MD104~~ V0827

C. Donor SSN or Employee I.D. No. 418 08 5702

D. Reason for Test: ☐ Pre-employment ☐ Random ☐ Reasonable Suspicion/Cause ☒ Post Accident ☐ Return to Duty ☐ Follow-up ☐ Other (specify)

E. Drug Tests to be Performed: ☒ THC, COC, PCP, OPI, AMP ☐ THC & COC Only ☐ Other (specify)

F. Collection Site Address: CWC - Fulton, 5070 Fulton Ind. — Address, City, State, Zip — Collector Phone No. 4043442930 — Collector Fax No. 4043448226S

STEP 2: COMPLETED BY COLLECTOR

Read specimen temperature within 4 minutes. Is temperature between 90° and 100° F? ☒ Yes ☐ No, Enter Remark

Specimen Collection: ☒ Split ☐ Single ☐ None Provided (Enter Remark) ☐ Observed (Enter Remark)

REMARKS

STEP 3: Collector affixes bottle seal(s) to bottle(s). Collector dates seal(s). Donor initials seal(s). Donor completes STEP 5 on Copy 2 (MRO Copy)

STEP 4: CHAIN OF CUSTODY - INITIATED BY COLLECTOR AND COMPLETED BY LABORATORY

I certify that the specimen given to me by the donor identified in the certification section on Copy 2 of this form was collected, labeled, sealed and released to the Delivery Service noted in accordance with applicable Federal requirements.

X (Signature of Collector) — (PRINT) Collector's Name (First, MI, Last): A. Boateng — Time of Collection 09:15 ☒ AM ☐ PM — Date (Mo/Day/Yr) 05/29/08

SPECIMEN BOTTLE(S) RELEASED TO: FedEx — Name of Delivery Service Transferring Specimen to Lab

RECEIVED AT LAB: X T. Thomas — (PRINT) Accessioner's Name (First, MI, Last) — Date (Mo/Day/Yr) 2008

Primary Specimen Bottle Seal Intact ☐ Yes ☐ No, Enter Remark Below

SPECIMEN BOTTLE(S) RELEASED TO: STORAGE B

STEP 5a: PRIMARY SPECIMEN TEST RESULTS - COMPLETED BY PRIMARY LABORATORY

☐ NEGATIVE ☒ POSITIVE for: ☒ MARIJUANA METABOLITE ☐ CODEINE ☐ AMPHETAMINE ☐ ADULTERATED
☐ DILUTE ☒ COCAINE METABOLITE ☐ MORPHINE ☐ METHAMPHETAMINE ☐ SUBSTITUTED
☐ REJECTED FOR TESTING ☐ PCP ☐ 6-ACETYLMORPHINE ☐ INVALID RESULT

REMARKS

TEST LAB (if different from above)

I certify that the specimen identified on this form was examined upon receipt, handled using chain of custody procedures, analyzed, and reported in accordance with applicable Federal requirements.

X (Signature of Certifying Scientist) — (PRINT) Certifying Scientist's Name (First, MI, Last): R. Tully — Date (Mo/Day/Yr) 6/13/08

STEP 5b: SPLIT SPECIMEN TEST RESULTS - (IF TESTED) COMPLETED BY SECONDARY LABORATORY

Laboratory Name — Laboratory Address

☐ RECONFIRMED ☐ FAILED TO RECONFIRM - REASON

I certify that the split specimen identified on this form was examined upon receipt, handled using chain of custody procedures, analyzed, and reported in accordance with applicable Federal requirements.

X Signature of Certifying Scientist — (PRINT) Certifying Scientist's Name (First, MI, Last) — Date (Mo/Day/Yr) / /

PRESS HARD - YOU ARE MAKING MULTIPLE COPIES

OMB No. 0930-0158

PEEL HERE

COPY 1 - LABORATORY

The second form is sent directly to the Medical Review Officer (MRO) from the collector of the sample and contains information on the driver. Once the MRO is informed of the positive test result, he completes the form with all information concerning the positive result.

Laboratory Form Completed by MRO

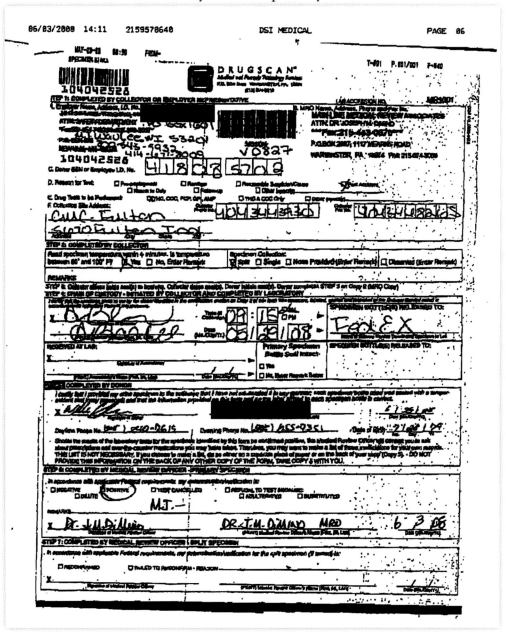

The MRO contacts the truck driver and attempts to determine if the truck driver has a medical reason for testing positive or has any explanation for the positive result. The MRO also offers the truck driver the opportunity to have a split specimen tested to determine if the first specimen was a false positive. The MRO completes an MRO worksheet to verify a positive test result including the results of the driver interview.

MRO Worksheet

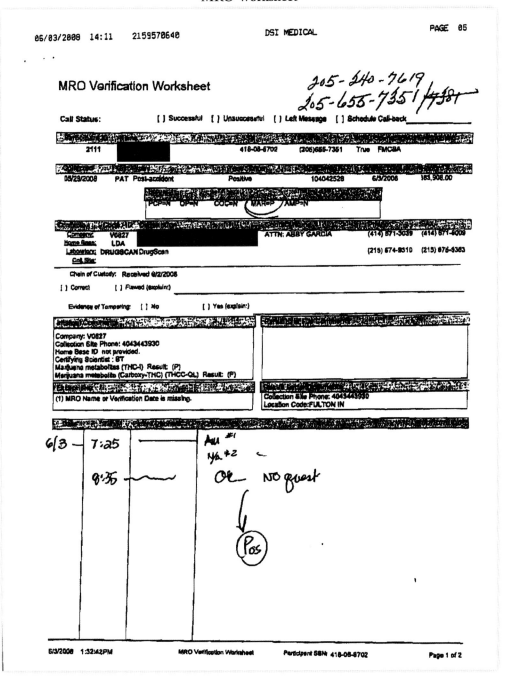

After speaking with the truck driver, the MRO determines if the outcome is considered positive under DOT guidelines. If the test is positive, a letter is sent to the trucking company informing them of the positive test result.

MRO Letter to Trucking Company

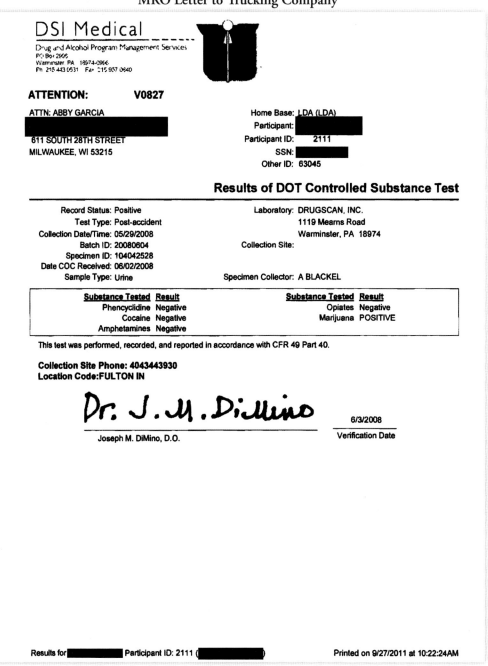

This driver tested positive for marijuana use.

**Practice Pointer: Obtain the MRO Worksheet to see what the driver told the MRO about the reason for the positive test result.

H. Admissibility of Post-Accident Testing Results

In every case where a truck driver tests positive for drugs or alcohol after a collision, there will be a question as to whether or not the test results are admissible. Because alcohol clears the system within hours, a positive alcohol test result is usually admissible.[297] It will be necessary to determine the driver's blood alcohol content (BAC) at the time of the collision. A toxicologist can take the BAC result at the point of post-accident testing and can calculate the BAC at the point of impact if the toxicologist is provided information as to the driver's weight and any food or drink consumed by the driver between the time of impact and the time of testing. Depending on the BAC at the point of impact, the toxicologist should be able to testify as to the amount of impairment caused by the alcohol in the driver's system and its effect on his ability to drive.

It is much more difficult to determine the admissibility of a positive drug screen. Marijuana, cocaine, amphetamines and most other drugs stay in the system for days instead of hours. Most drug screens do not indicate the amount of the drug in the system with the specificity to determine when the drug was consumed. Because drugs only cause impairment for hours but stay in the system for days, the defense will argue that the truck driver had taken the drug days before the collision and was not impaired at the time of the collision even though he tested positive. Unless there is witness testimony that the driver was acting erratically at the scene, acted like he was on drugs or there is some other evidence of drug use at the scene, expert testimony will be required to show that the positive test result equals impairment at the time of the collision in order for the test result to be admissible.[298]

Similarly, a failure to conduct a post-accident drug or alcohol screen is usually only admissible if there is evidence that the driver was acting erratically, smelled of alcohol or drugs or had some evidence of alcohol or drug use at the scene.[299]

I. Refusal to Submit to Testing

Any person who holds a commercial driver's license or drives a commercial vehicle is deemed to have consented to alcohol and controlled substances testing as required by federal regulations.[300] A trucking company is prohibited from allowing a driver who refuses to submit to testing to perform or continue to perform a safety sensitive function.[301] Refusal to submit means that the driver (1) fails to provide adequate breath upon request for an alcohol test without a valid medical explanation, (2) fails to provide an adequate urine sample upon request for controlled substance testing or (3) engages in conduct that clearly obstructs the testing process.[302]

J. Alcohol & Controlled Substance Testing Policies and Procedures

Alcohol and controlled substance testing must comply with federal regulations dictating the proper methods of taking and preserving samples and performing the tests.[303] A driver may be terminated for failure to pass a drug or alcohol test[304] as long as the motor carrier's drug testing program meets federal specifications.[305] A carrier may retain an independent agency to perform the actual testing on the drivers. If the agency fails to conduct the testing in an appropriate manner, the carrier cannot be held liable for the agency's actions.[306] A motor carrier may also enforce alcohol and controlled substances policies and procedures that are more stringent than the guidelines contained in the federal regulations.[307]

---

[297] Frederick v. Swift Transportation Co., Inc., 591 F.Supp.2d 1149 (2008).
[298] Bedford v. Moore, 166 S.W.3d 454 (Tx. 2005); Frederick v. Swift Transportation Co., Inc., 591 F.Supp.2d 1149 (2008).
[299] Abdul v. Logistics Express, 2009 WL 6965088 (S.D.Miss. 2009).
[300] 49 C.F.R. § 383.72.
[301] 49 C.F.R. § 382.211.
[302] 49 C.F.R. § 382.107.
[303] 49 C.F.R. § 382.105.
[304] Exxon Corporation v. Esso Workers' Union, Inc., 118 F.3d 841 (1997).
[305] Reames v. Department of Public Works, 707 A.2d 1377 (N.J. Super. 1998).
[306] Carroll v. Federal Express Corporation, 113 F.3d 163 (9th Cir. 1997).
[307] 49 C.F.R. § 382.111.

K. Rehabilitation

A trucking company must inform a driver who violates the alcohol or controlled substances prohibitions of the resources available to assist him in evaluating and resolving problems associated with alcohol and controlled substances abuse.[308] The driver must then be evaluated by a substance abuse professional to determine the kind of assistance needed for his rehabilitation.[309] A carrier must ensure that a driver who is in need of assistance in resolving problems associated with alcohol misuse and/or use of controlled substances is subject to unannounced follow up testing as directed by a substance abuse professional.[310] The driver shall also be routinely evaluated by a substance abuse professional to make sure the driver complies with his treatment plan.[311] Before a driver who has violated the alcohol prohibitions can return to duty requiring the performance of a safety-sensitive function, the driver must be given an alcohol test with a result less than 0.02 blood alcohol concentration.[312] A driver must take a controlled substances test indicating a verified negative result for controlled substances use before he can return to work after a violation of the controlled substance guidelines.[313] The carrier does not have to provide referral, evaluation, and rehabilitation services to a driver if the violation is discovered as a result of pre-employment testing.[314]

L. Retention & Disclosure of Records

A motor carrier must retain for five years: (1) driver alcohol test results indicating an alcohol concentration of 0.02 or greater; (2) any verified positive controlled substance test results; (3) documentation of refusals to submit to alcohol or controlled substance testing; and (4) evaluations and referrals to rehabilitation specialists.[315] The carrier must retain for one year any records of negative and canceled controlled substances test results and alcohol test results with a result of less than 0.02.[316] All records regarding the training of drivers and supervisors must be maintained during the time of their employment and for an additional two years.[317] Carriers are also required generally to maintain any documents (1) related to random drug testing, (2) generated in connection with decisions to administer reasonable suspicion alcohol or controlled substances tests, (3) generated in connection with post-accident tests, (4) related to a refusal to submit to testing, (5) generated in connection with verifications of a driver's testing from prior employers, (6) related to a driver's evaluation and consultation with a substance abuse professional and (7) related to educational or training materials provided to drivers including the carrier's testing policies and procedures.[318] A trucking company must prepare and maintain a summary of its alcohol and controlled substances testing results for the previous calendar year when requested by the Secretary of Transportation, any DOT agency, or any State or local officials with regulatory authority over the company or its drivers.[319]

Documents regarding testing of a driver may only be released by consent of the driver, by request of the National Transportation Safety Board, by request of a subsequent employer with the consent of the driver, by request of Secretary of Transportation, any DOT agency, or any State or local officials with regulatory authority over the carrier or its drivers or in conjunction with an action for benefits sought by a driver.[320] In a civil action, the results of a drug or alcohol test can only be released if the driver consents to production or if a court of competent jurisdiction determines the information

---

[308] 49 C.F.R. § 382.605(a).
[309] 49 C.F.R. § 382.605(b).
[310] 49 C.F.R. § 382.311(a).
[311] 49 C.F.R. § 382.605(c)(2).
[312] 49 C.F.R. § 382.309(a).
[313] 49 C.F.R. § 382.309(b).
[314] 49 C.F.R. § 382.605(f).
[315] 49 C.F.R. § 382.401(b)(1).
[316] 49 C.F.R. § 382.401(b)(3).
[317] 49 C.F.R. § 382.401(b)(4).
[318] 49 C.F.R. § 382.401(c).
[319] 49 C.F.R. § 382.403.
[320] 49 C.F.R. § 382.405.

sought is relevant and issues an order directing the company to produce the results.[321] The results may only be released with a binding stipulation that the documentation will only be made available to the parties to the litigation.[322]

---

[321] 49 C.F.R. § 40.323(a).
[322] 49 C.F.R. § 40.323(b).

VI. Hours of Service Regulations

A. Maximum Hours of Service

A driver carrying property cannot drive more than 11 hours following 10 consecutive hours off-duty.[323] A driver cannot operate a commercial vehicle for any period after having been on duty 14 hours following 10 consecutive hours off-duty.[324] A driver carrying passengers cannot drive more than 10 hours following 8 consecutive hours off-duty or operate a commercial vehicle for any period after having been on duty 15 hours following 8 consecutive hours off-duty.[325] A driver cannot operate a commercial vehicle after having been on duty 60 hours in any 7 consecutive days if the employing motor carrier does not operate commercial motor vehicles every day of the week and cannot operate a commercial vehicle after having been on duty 70 hours in any consecutive 8 days if the employing motor carrier operates commercial vehicles every day.[326] Any period of 34 consecutive off duty hours will reset the 7 or 8 consecutive days[327] A driver with a sleeper berth in his vehicle must have at least 10 consecutive hours either in his sleeper berth or off duty or some combination of the two before beginning to drive.[328]

On duty time means all time from the time a driver begins to work or is required to be in readiness to work until the driver is relieved from work including: (1) all time at a plant, terminal, facility or other property waiting to be dispatched, unless the driver has been relieved of duty by the carrier; (2) all time inspecting, servicing, or conditioning any commercial vehicle; (3) all time spent at the driving controls of a commercial vehicle in operation; (4) all time in or upon a commercial vehicle, except in the sleeper berth; (5) all time loading or unloading a commercial vehicle, supervising or assisting in the loading or unloading, attending a vehicle being loaded or unloaded, remaining in readiness to operate the commercial vehicle or in giving or receiving receipts for shipments loaded or unloaded; (6) all time repairing, obtaining assistance or remaining in attendance upon a disabled vehicle; (7) all time spent providing a breath or urine sample, including travel time, to perform a test required by federal regulations; (8) all time performing any work on behalf of the motor carrier and (9) all time performing compensated work for any person or entity.[329] When a driver at the direction of the motor carrier is traveling, but not driving or assuming any other responsibility to the carrier, such time shall be counted as on duty time unless the driver is afforded at least 10 consecutive hours off duty when arriving at his destination, in which case he shall be considered off duty for the entire period.[330] A motor carrier may not permit a driver to operate a commercial vehicle in violation of the maximum hours of service.[331]

Practice Pointer: Retain a qualified expert to examine the steps taken by the trucking company to monitor a driver's hours of service.

B. Exceptions to Hours of Service Requirements

A driver who encounters adverse driving conditions and cannot safely complete his run within the required maximum driving time may drive an additional 2 hours to complete the run or reach a place of safety.[332] In case of an emergency, a driver may also complete his run without being in violation of the maximum hours of service if the driver could have reasonably completed the run absent the emergency.[333] The maximum hours of service requirements do not apply to a driver-salesperson who

---

[323] 49 C.F.R. § 395.3(a).
[324] 49 C.F.R. § 395.3(a).
[325] 49 C.F.R. § 395.5(a).
[326] 49 C.F.R. § 395.3(b) & 395.5(b).
[327] 49 C.F.R. § 395.3(c).
[328] 49 C.F.R. § 395.1(g).
[329] 49 C.F.R. § 395.2.
[330] 49 C.F.R. § 395.1(j).
[331] 49 C.F.R. § 395.3.
[332] 49 C.F.R. § 395.1(b)(1).
[333] 49 C.F.R. § 395.1(b)(2).

drives less than 40 hours in any period of 7 consecutive days.[334] The regulations also do not apply to drivers of commercial vehicles engaged solely in making local deliveries to the ultimate consumer during the Christmas holidays from December 10th to 25th,[335] and the transportation of agricultural commodities within a 100 mile radius during planting or harvesting seasons.[336]

Practice Pointer: Exempt employees are required to keep information about their hours of service although they do not have to keep driver's logs.

C. Driver's Logs

A driver must record his duty status for each 24-hour period on an electronic log computer system in the tractor that is provided by his employer.[337]

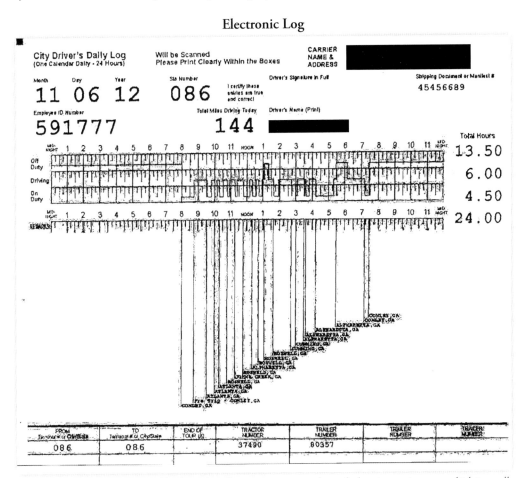

This log is automatically generated by the on-board computer system and must be kept in one time zone which is usually the home terminal of the driver.

The driver's duty status must be recorded as (1) "Off duty" or "Off", (2) "Sleeper Berth" or "SB", (3) "Driving" or "D", (4) "On-duty not driving" or "On."[338] The electronic log must identify the city, town or place where any change of status occurs.[339] The log must identify the total miles driven

---

[334] 49 C.F.R. § 395.1(c).
[335] 49 C.F.R. § 395.1(f).
[336] 49 C.F.R. § 395.1(k).
[337] 49 C.F.R. § 395.8(a)(1).
[338] 49 C.F.R. § 395.8(b).
[339] 49 C.F.R. § 395.8(c).

per day and the total hours on duty.[340] The electronic log must be retrievable on demand through the computer system in the tractor.[341] If the driver uses a handwritten log, the driver must complete all entries legibly and in his own handwriting.[342]

The requirement for keeping daily logs does not apply to drivers who operate within a 100-mile radius of the normal work reporting location if the driver is released from work within 12 consecutive hours, has at least 10 hours off-duty time, does not exceed 11 hours maximum driving time, and the trucking company maintains accurate and true time records of the driver's work for a period of six months.[343]

A motor carrier, when using a driver for the first time, must obtain a signed statement from the driver giving the total time on duty during the immediately preceding 7 days.[344] When a driver works for more than one carrier, he must have logs with each carrier with entries indicating both his status and the carrier he served during that period.[345] A motor carrier must maintain records of duty status and all supporting documents for each driver it employs for a period of six months from the date of receipt.[346] A driver must retain a copy of each handwritten log for the previous 7 consecutive days which shall be in his possession and available for inspection while on duty.[347]

A motor carrier must monitor its drivers to ensure compliance with the provisions regarding recording his duty status time.[348] A carrier's destruction of driver's logs or related documents may give rise to a presumption that the evidence was not preserved because it was unfavorable to the carrier and, therefore, that the driver must have violated the federal regulations.[349] A driver cannot be forced to testify about his violation of the hours of service regulations over a Fifth Amendment objection since he would be subject to prosecution for any violation.[350] However, driver's logs are not documents protected by the 5th Amendment privilege since the driver is required by law to maintain the logs.[351]

---

[340] 49 C.F.R. § 395.8(d).
[341] 49 C.F.R. § 395.15.
[342] 49 C.F.R. § 395.8(e).
[343] 49 C.F.R. § 395.1(e).
[344] 49 C.F.R. § 395.8(j)(2).
[345] 49 C.F.R. § 395.8(j)(1).
[346] 49 C.F.R. § 395.8(k)(1).
[347] 49 C.F.R. § 395.8(k)(2).
[348] 49 C.F.R. § 395.8(a).
[349] J.B. Hunt Transport, Inc. v. Bentley, 427 S.E.2d 499 (Ga. 1993).
[350] Thomas v. Tyler, 841 F.Supp. 1119 (D.Kansas 1993).
[351] Id.

Bill of Lading

We have used bills of lading to show that a driver's logs are inaccurate because the logs do not match the bills of lading.

**Practice Pointer: Request not only the eight days of driver's logs from before the accident but also any bills of lading, weight tickets, hotel receipts and other similar documents needed to verify the accuracy of the driver's logs.

D. Violations of Hours of Service Provisions

A driver will be declared out of service if he drives after being on duty in excess of the maximum periods or if he fails to have a record of duty status current on the day of examination and for the prior 7 consecutive days.[352] A carrier may not allow a driver who has been declared out of service for violating the maximum hours regulations to operate a motor vehicle until he may lawfully do so under the rules.[353] A driver who has been declared out of service for failure to prepare a record of duty status cannot operate a commercial vehicle until he has been off duty for 10 consecutive hours.[354] A driver must notify the carrier within 24 hours of being placed out of service for such a violation.[355]

**Practice Pointer: Request information about prior violations of hours of service regulations by the motor carrier and its drivers.

---

[352] 49 C.F.R. § 395.13(b).
[353] 49 C.F.R. § 395.13(c)(1).
[354] 49 C.F.R. § 395.13(c)(1).
[355] 49 C.F.R. § 395.13(d)(3).

VII. Federal Motor Carrier Safety Regulations

The FMCSR are applicable to all employers, employees, and commercial motor vehicles which transport property or passengers in interstate commerce.[356] Whether transportation is interstate or intrastate is determined by the essential character of the commerce, manifested by a shipper's fixed and persisting intent at the time of the shipment which is ascertainable from all the facts and circumstances surrounding the transportation scheme.[357] The central focus in this inquiry is whether or not the ultimate destination of the shipment is identified as a location outside the state at the time the transportation is arranged.[358] By statute, a State may require carriers involved in intrastate transportation or hauling exempt commodities to comply with the FMCSR.[359]

The FMCSR are minimum standards for commercial vehicles.[360] Every interstate motor carrier and driver must be familiar with and comply with the standards contained in the FMCSR.[361] A motor carrier cannot allow a vehicle to be operated unless it meets the minimum standards set forth in the FMCSR.[362] Motor carriers are required to make sure all drivers comply with the provisions of the FMCSR.[363] No one can aid, abet, encourage or require a motor carrier or driver to violate the FMCSR.[364]

**Practice Pointer: If the trucking company operates as an intrastate carrier, review state law to determine if the state has adopted the FMCSR as applicable to all operations in the state.

A. Exemptions to the FMCSR

The FMCSR do not apply to (1) motor vehicles transporting only school children and teachers to or from school, (2) motor vehicles providing taxicab services, (3) motor vehicles operated by or for a hotel to transport hotel patrons between the hotel and a local station, (4) motor vehicles controlled and operated by a farmer and transporting the farmer's agricultural products or supplies to the farm, (5) transportation of ordinary livestock, agricultural or horticultural commodities, (6) motor vehicles used to distribute newspapers, (7) transportation of passengers or property incidental to transportation by aircraft or transportation of property by motor carrier because of adverse weather conditions or mechanical failure of the aircraft, (8) the operation of a motor vehicle in a national park or monument, (9) motor vehicles carrying less than 15 passengers to and from work, (10) transportation of used pallets and empty shipping containers, (11) transportation of natural, crushed or vesicular rock to be used for decorative purposes, wood chips, or broken, crushed or powdered glass, (12) transportation entirely within a municipality or in a commercial zone adjacent to a municipality unless part of a continuous carriage from outside the municipality or zone, (13) transportation by motor vehicle provided casually, occasionally, or reciprocally but not as a regular occupation or business.[365] An entity engaged in a business other than transportation for hire does not have to comply with the FMCSR.[366] The FMCSR do not apply to a company that hires an independent contractor to transport goods when the company is not in the transportation business.[367]

---

[356] 49 C.F.R. § 390.3(a).
[357] Progressive Casualty Insurance Co. v. Hoover, 768 A.2d 1157 (Penn. 2001); Southern Pacific Transportation Co. v. Interstate Commerce Commission, 565 F.2d 615 (9th Cir. 1977).
[358] Pittsburgh-Johnstown-Altoona Express, Inc. v. Pennsylvania Public Utility Commission, 554 A.2d 137 (Penn. 1989); Progressive Casualty Insurance Co. v. Hoover, 768 A.2d 1157 (Penn. 2001).
[359] Schmidt v. Royer, 574 N.W.2d 618 (S.D. 1998).
[360] 49 C.F.R. § 393.1(a).
[361] 49 C.F.R. § 393.1(b).
[362] 49 C.F.R. § 393.1(b).
[363] 49 C.F.R. § 390.11.
[364] 49 C.F.R. § 390.13.
[365] 49 U.S.C. § 13506; 49 C.F.R. § 372.101.
[366] 49 U.S.C. § 13505.
[367] Ek v. Herrington, 939 F.2d 839 (9th Cir. 1991).

B. Non-Exempt Commodities

Although agricultural products are generally exempt from the FMCSR, by statute, the transportation of the following products are NOT exempt from the FMCSR: animal fats, butter, canned fruits and vegetables, carnauba wax, charcoal, cheese, coal, cocoa beans, coffee beans, cotton yarn, diatomaceous earth, frozen dinners, alfalfa pellets, certain feeds, fertilizer, fish, flagstone, flour, forest resin products such as turpentine, certain fruits and berries, popped popcorn, precooked rice, wheat germ, gravel, any product of a slaughtered animal, hay sweetened with molasses, hemp fiber, green and salted hides, insecticides, limestone, monkeys, race horses, show horses, zoo animals, lumber (rough sawed or plain), maple syrup, certain meals, meat and meat products (fresh, frozen, or canned), milk and cream (condensed or sterilized in hermetically sealed cans), chocolate, molasses, roasted or boiled peanuts, certain oils, racing pigeons, beet pulp, sugar cane pulp, rock (except to be used for decorative purposes), rubber, sand, potting soil, top soil, frozen soup, sugar, cane syrup, maple syrup, tea, cigars and cigarettes, smoking tobacco, french fried potatoes, and wool products.[368]

C. Definition of Commercial Vehicles

The FMCSR applies to all commercial vehicles.[369] A commercial vehicle is defined as any vehicle used on the highway in interstate commerce transporting people or property with a gross vehicle weight rating (GVWR) or gross combination weight rating or gross vehicle weight rating or gross combination weight of 10,001 lbs. or more.[370] Transporting property means carrying any tools or equipment as part of a commercial enterprise.[371] Most states have adopted the FMCSR and its definition of a commercial vehicle as applicable to any vehicles involved in intrastate commerce. The end result is that the owner and/or operator of any business vehicle and/or trailer with any load which in combination weighs more than 10,001 lbs. must comply with all the FMCSR. Straight trucks, work vans, large pickup trucks with trailers, landscaping vehicles, HVAC work vehicles, plumbing trucks and utility trucks may fall within this definition of a commercial vehicle.

**Practice Pointer: Identify the weight of the vehicle, trailer and equipment in a vehicle smaller than a tractor trailer to see if it meets the definition of a commercial vehicle.

D. Compliance with State Law

According to the provisions of the FMCSR, every commercial motor vehicle must be operated in accordance with the laws, ordinances, and regulations of the State or jurisdiction in which it is being operated unless the FHWA imposes a higher standard of care in which case the federal regulation must be complied with.[372] States cannot pass any law, rule or regulation relating to rates, routes or services of any motor carrier[373] except that state government may impose highway route controls or limitations based on the size or weight of a motor vehicle or the hazardous nature of cargo[374] and may also mandate minimum amounts of insurance in order to operate on state highways.[375]

---

[368] 49 C.F.R. § 372.115.
[369] 49 C.F.R. § 390.3.
[370] 49 C.F.R. § 390.5.
[371] Midwest Crane and Rigging, Inc. v. FMCSA, 603 F.3d 837 (10th Cir. 2010); Friedrich v. U.S. Computer Services, 974 F.2d 409 (3rd Cir. 1992).
[372] 49 C.F.R. § 392.2.
[373] 49 U.S.C. § 14501(c).
[374] 49 U.S.C. § 14501.
[375] 49 U.S.C. § 14501.

E. Designating Unsafe Vehicles as Out-of-Service

A vehicle cannot be operated in such a manner as to likely cause an accident or breakdown of the vehicle except that a vehicle discovered in an unsafe condition may be driven to the nearest place where repairs can safely be performed.[376] The FHWA routinely inspects commercial vehicles and will declare out-of-service any vehicle which by reason of its mechanical condition or loading would likely cause an accident or a breakdown of the vehicle.[377]

DOT Post-Accident Inspection

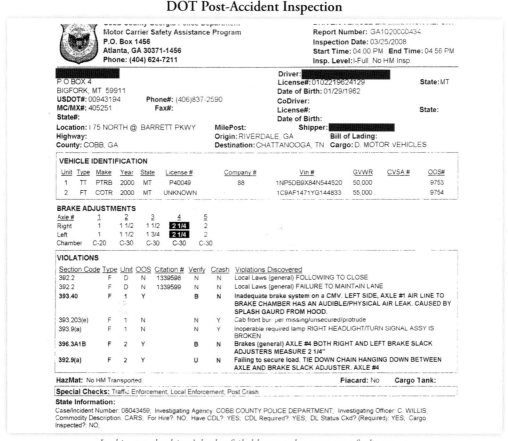

In this case, the driver's brakes failed because they were out of adjustment.

FHWA inspectors must record the results of any Driver Equipment Compliance Check[378] and place an out-of-service sticker an any vehicle which fails an inspection.[379] A vehicle marked out-of-service may not be operated until all repairs required by the out-of-service notice have been satisfactorily completed.[380] No person may remove an out-of-service sticker prior to completion of the repairs required by the out-of-service notice.[381] A driver must deliver an inspection report at his next stop at the carrier's terminal or facility.[382] If the driver is not scheduled to stop at a terminal or facility within 24 hours of receipt of an inspection report, then the driver must immediately mail a copy of the report to the motor carrier.[383] A carrier must certify to the FHWA within 15 days of the

---

[376] 49 C.F.R. § 396.7.
[377] 49 C.F.R. § 396.9(c).
[378] 49 C.F.R. § 396.9(b).
[379] 49 C.F.R. § 396.9(c)(1).
[380] 49 C.F.R. § 396.9(c).
[381] 49 C.F.R. § 396.9(c)(3).
[382] 49 C.F.R. § 396.9(d).
[383] 49 C.F.R. § 396.9(d).

inspection that all violations noted in the report have been corrected and retain a copy of the report for one year from the date of the inspection.[384]

F. Unsafe Dispatch

A motor carrier cannot schedule a run or require the operation of a commercial vehicle between points in such period of time as would necessitate the vehicle being operated at speeds greater than those prescribed by the jurisdictions in or through which the vehicle is being operated.[385]

Practice Pointer: Compare bills of lading and driver logs to determine the average speed of the driver on his runs.

G. Pre-Trip Inspections & End of Day Reports

A driver cannot operate a commercial motor vehicle until he has inspected the following parts and satisfied himself that the parts are in good working order: (1) Service brakes including trailer brake connections, (2) Parking brakes, (3) Steering mechanism, (4) Lighting devices and reflectors, (5) Tires, (6) Horn, (7) Windshield wipers, (8) Rear vision mirrors, and (9) Coupling devices.[386] A driver must also inspect and be satisfied that all emergency equipment is working properly.[387] Before operating a vehicle, a driver must be satisfied that the vehicle is in safe operating condition, review the last driver vehicle inspection report, and if defects were noted and repaired, sign the report.[388]

Every driver must prepare a report in writing at the completion of each day on each vehicle operated by the driver concerning the condition of the same parts and accessories examined during the pre-trip inspection.[389] However, the driver does not have to complete an end-of-day report if he finds no defects with the vehicle.[390]

---

[384] 49 C.F.R. § 396.9(3).
[385] 49 C.F.R. § 392.6.
[386] 49 C.F.R. § 392.7.
[387] 49 C.F.R. § 392.8.
[388] 49 C.F.R. § 396.13.
[389] 49 C.F.R. § 396.11(a).
[390] 49 C.F.R. § 396.11(b).

Daily Inspection Report

The driver no longer has to complete a Daily Inspection Report if there are no defects.

Since there is no longer a requirement to complete a report if no defects are found, it will be impossible to differentiate if the driver failed to do the inspection versus simply not finding anything wrong when he did the inspection.

If a driver does find a defect, the report must identify the vehicle and list any defect which would affect the safe operation of the vehicle or result in its mechanical breakdown.[391] The driver must sign the report and must complete a report for each vehicle operated during the workday.[392] Prior to requiring or permitting a driver to operate a vehicle, the motor carrier must examine the driver's report and repair any defect which would likely affect the safe operation of the vehicle.[393] The original

---

[391] 49 C.F.R. § 396.11(b).
[392] 49 C.F.R. § 396.11(b).
[393] 49 C.F.R. § 396.11(c).

driver inspection report and the certification of any repairs performed to correct the defects identified in the report must be retained for three months from the date the report was prepared.[394]

Practice Pointer: Request copies of all daily inspection reports for the three-month period preceding the accident.

H. Annual Inspections

A commercial vehicle must undergo an annual inspection at least once during the preceding 12-month period, and an annual inspection report must be kept with the vehicle.[395]

---

[394] 49 C.F.R. § 396.11(c)(2).
[395] 49 C.F.R. § 396.17(c).

Annual Inspection

In lieu of an annual inspection, the motor carrier can rely on an inspection performed by the DOT or a state governmental entity that includes an inspection of the same mechanical parts required for the annual inspection.[396] The trucking company may perform the inspection itself or choose to have a commercial garage, leasing company, truck stop, or other similar commercial business perform the inspection.[397] A periodic inspection performed by an FHWA agent may substitute for the annual inspection as long as the FHWA inspection meets the minimum standards for annual inspections.[398] A motor carrier must insure that any work performed on the brakes of a commercial

---

[396] 49 C.F.R. § 396.17.
[397] 49 C.F.R. § 396.17(d)-(e).
[398] 49 C.F.R. § 396.23.

vehicle, including all inspections, maintenance, service or repairs to the brakes, is completed by a qualified brake inspector who has completed an apprenticeship program and has brake-related experience and training of at least one year.[399]

Practice Pointer: Request a copy of the annual inspection report covering the date of the accident.

I. Accident Register

For accidents that occur after April 29, 2003, trucking companies are required to maintain an accident register listing information about each accident involving its drivers for a three year period.[400] The accident register must contain the following information for each accident: (1) the date of the accident, (2) the city and state where the accident occurred, (3) the driver's name, (4) the number of injuries, (5) the number of fatalities, and (6) the involvement of hazardous materials.[401] The company must also keep copies of all accident reports generated by or on behalf of State or other governmental entities or insurers for each accident listed on the accident register.[402] Information contained on the accident register is discoverable although attorney notes in investigative files on each accident may be subject to the work product privilege.[403]

Practice Pointer: Request a copy of the accident register for the three year period preceding the accident and any related documentation.

J. Loading Procedures

Commercial vehicles must be loaded in such a manner as to prevent its cargo from leaking, spilling, blowing or falling from the vehicle.[404] The cargo must be immobilized or secured to prevent shifting to the extent that the vehicle's stability or maneuverability is affected.[405] All vehicle structures, systems, parts and components used to secure cargo must be in proper working order with no damaged or weakened components that will adversely affect their performance.[406] Cargo must be firmly immobilized or secured on or within a vehicle by structures of adequate strength, dunnage or dunnage bags, shoring bars, tiedowns or a combination of these.[407] Articles of cargo that are likely to roll must be restrained by chocks, wedges, a cradle or equivalent means to prevent rolling.[408] Federal regulations provide for specific means of securing logs,[409] building products,[410] metal coils,[411] paper rolls,[412] concrete pipes,[413] intermodal containers,[414] automobiles,[415] heavy equipment,[416] crushed vehicles,[417] and boulders.[418] Cargo must be secured so that when a vehicle decelerates at a rate of 20 feet per second, the cargo will remain on the vehicle and will not penetrate the vehicle's front-end structure.[419] Any vehicle having a load or component which extends beyond the sides more than 4 inches or more than 4 feet beyond the rear must have the extremities marked with a red or orange

---

[399] 49 C.F.R. 396.25.
[400] 49 C.F.R. § 390.15(b).
[401] 49 C.F.R. § 390.15(b).
[402] 49 C.F.R. § 390.15(b).
[403] Gruenbaum v. Werner Enterprises, Inc., 270 F.R.D. 298 (S.D. Ohio 2010).
[404] 49 C.F.R. § 393.100(b).
[405] 49 C.F.R. § 393.100(c).
[406] 49 C.F.R. § 393.104(b).
[407] 49 C.F.R. § 393.106(b).
[408] 49 C.F.R. § 393.106(c).
[409] 49 C.F.R. § 393.116.
[410] 49 C.F.R. § 393.118.
[411] 49 C.F.R. § 393.120.
[412] 49 C.F.R. § 393.122.
[413] 49 C.F.R. § 393.124.
[414] 49 C.F.R. § 393.126.
[415] 49 C.F.R. § 393.128.
[416] 49 C.F.R. § 393.130.
[417] 49 C.F.R. § 393.132.
[418] 49 C.F.R. § 393.136.
[419] 49 C.F.R. § 393.114(d).

fluorescent warning flag.[420] If the projecting load is 2 feet in width or less, then only one flag is required at the extreme rear of the load.[421] If the projecting load is greater than 2 feet in width, two flags must be used at the extreme width and length on each side of the load.[422]

K. Responsibilities for Proper Loading

A driver cannot operate a commercial vehicle unless (1) the cargo is properly distributed and adequately secured, (2) the means of fastening the cargo is secured, and (3) the cargo does not obscure the driver's view or interfere with the movement of his arms or legs.[423] A driver must assure himself that the load is adequately secured before he drives the vehicle and must examine the cargo and its load-securing devices within the first 50 miles after beginning a trip and adjust the load-securing devices as needed.[424] The driver must also reexamine the cargo and its securing devices when he makes a change of his duty status, after the vehicle has been driven for three hours, or after the vehicle has been driven 150 miles whichever comes first.[425] The load inspection procedures do not apply to a sealed trailer when the driver has been ordered not to open it or to a trailer that has been loaded in a manner that makes inspection of the cargo impracticable.[426]

If a member of the public is injured because of improperly loaded cargo, both the shipper who loaded the cargo and the carrier may be held liable for the injury.[427] A shipper that assumes responsibility for loading the vehicle can be held liable for improperly securing a load under a common law theory of negligence, and federal regulations will provide evidence of the proper standard of care to be utilized by the shipper in loading the vehicle.[428] When the driver himself is injured in an accident, the shipper cannot be held liable for the improper loading of the vehicle unless the loading defects are latent and concealed and cannot be discerned by ordinary observation by the agents of the carrier.[429] In determining if the defect in loading is patent and should have been discovered by the driver, a court will take into consideration the experience of the driver[430] and whether the driver is given assurances by the shipper's employees that there is no defect in the loading of the cargo.[431] A motor carrier cannot be held liable for improperly loading a sealed trailer since the driver does not have the opportunity to inspect the load.[432] When a person is injured during the loading or unloading process at the shipper or consignee's facility, the trucking company's liability will be determined according to the rules applicable to the facility owner, and the company will be subject to the same liability or freedom from liability as the owner.[433]

Practice Pointer: Consider a cause of action against the entity that loaded the vehicle in addition to the trucking company.

---

[420] 49 C.F.R. § 393.87.
[421] 49 C.F.R. § 393.87(b).
[422] 49 C.F.R. § 393.87(b).
[423] 49 C.F.R. § 392.9(a).
[424] 49 C.F.R. § 392.9(b)(2).
[425] 49 C.F.R. § 392.9(b)(3).
[426] 49 C.F.R. § 392.9(b)(4).
[427] Burke v. J.F. Allen Company, 182 F.3d 907 (W.Va. 1999); Skeie v. Mercer Trucking Co., Inc., 61 P.3d 1207 (Wash. 2003); Fortner v. Tecchio Trucking, Inc., 597 F.Supp.2d 755 (E.D.Tenn. 2009); Bujnoch v. National Oilwell Barco, L.P., 542 S.W.3d 2 (Tx. 2018).
[428] Reed v. Ace Doran Hauling & Rigging Co., 1997 WL 177849 (N.D. Ill. 1997); Symington v. Great Western Trucking Co., Inc., 668 F.Supp. 1278 (S.D. Iowa 1987); Locicero v. Interpace Corp., 266 N.W.2d 423 (Wis. 1978).
[429] Decker v. New England Public Warehouse, Inc., 749 A.2d 762 (Maine 2000); Fontanne v. Federal Paper Board Co., Inc., 434 N.E.2d 331 (Ill. 1982).
[430] Alitalia v. Arrow Trucking Co., 977 F.Supp. 973 (D.Ariz. 1997).
[431] Franklin Stainless Corp. v. Marlo Transportation Corp., 748 F.2d 865 (4th Cir. 1984); Ebasco Services, Inc. v. Pacific Intermountain Express Co., 398 F.Supp. 565 (S.D.N.Y. 1975).
[432] Miller v. Rollins Leasing Corp., 1999 WL 739539 (Ohio 1999).
[433] Zuniga v. Pay Less Drug Stores, N.W., Inc., 917 P.2d 584 (Wash. 1996); Taylor v. Duke, 713 N.E.2d 877 (Ind. 1999).

L. Stopped Tractor-Trailers & Warning Devices

A vehicle must be equipped with three bi-directional emergency reflective triangles or at least 6 fusees or 3 liquid-burning flares.[434] Liquid-burning flares, fusees, oil lanterns, or any signal produced by a flame shall not be carried on a commercial vehicle transporting hazardous materials, flammable gas, or flammable liquid whether loaded or empty.[435] Whenever a commercial vehicle is stopped upon the traveled portion of a highway or the shoulder of a highway, the driver of the stopped vehicle shall immediately activate the hazard warning flashers and continue the flashing until the driver places warning devices next to the unit.[436]

The driver must place warning devices as soon as possible after stopping his vehicle, but in any case no less than 10 minutes, at the following points: (1) 10 feet away from the vehicle in the direction of approaching traffic, (2) 100 feet away from the vehicle in the center of the traffic lane or the shoulder of the road occupied by the vehicle in the direction of approaching traffic, and (3) 100 feet away from the vehicle in the direction away from approaching traffic.[437] The placement of warning devices is not required within the business or residential district of a municipality except at night or times when highway lighting is insufficient to make a vehicle discernible at a distance of 500 feet.[438] If a vehicle is stopped within 500 feet of a curve, crest of a hill or other obstruction to view, the driver shall place a warning signal up to 500 feet in the direction of the obstruction to give ample warning to other drivers.[439] If the vehicle is stopped on a divided or one-way highway, the driver must place one warning device at a distance of 200 feet and one warning device at a distance of 100 feet in a direction toward approaching traffic and one warning device within 10 feet of the rear of the vehicle.[440] The requirements for activating flashers and placing warning markers is not applicable to business and residential districts during daylight hours.[441]

Warning Triangles

Most truck drivers use warning triangles to alert a motorist approaching from the rear.

---

[434] 49 C.F.R. § 393.95(f)(2).
[435] 49 C.F.R. § 393.95(g).
[436] 49 C.F.R. § 392.22(a).
[437] 49 C.F.R. § 392.22(b)(1).
[438] 49 C.F.R. § 392.22(b)(2).
[439] 49 C.F.R. § 392.22(b)(2).
[440] 49 C.F.R. § 392.22(b)(2).
[441] Merzigian v. Sunbury Transport, Ltd., 523 F.Supp.2d 116 (D.Mass. 2007).

If gasoline or other flammable liquid leaks from a stopped vehicle, no emergency signal producing a flame shall be lighted or placed except at such a distance as will assure the prevention of a fire or explosion.[442] A lighted fusee or other flame-producing emergency signal cannot be attached to any part of the commercial vehicle.[443] Flame producing emergency signals cannot be used for any commercial vehicle transporting explosive material, any cargo tank vehicle used for the transportation of flammable, explosive or poisonous material (whether loaded or empty), and instead a driver must use emergency reflective triangles, red electric lanterns or red emergency reflectors.[444]

If a tractor-trailer driver stops on the shoulder of the road, without an emergency mechanical breakdown, then the trucking company can be held liable when a vehicle leaves the lanes of travel and strikes the rear of the trailer because it is foreseeable that traffic will go onto the shoulder of the road and hit a vehicle that is illegally parked there.[445] When an injured party's vehicle collides with a stopped tractor-trailer and the truck driver failed to immediately activate his flashers[446] before exiting the vehicle or failed to place warning signals or devices in place, the federal regulations requiring the use of flashers and the placement of warning signals near the vehicle can be used to establish the carrier's negligence.[447] A carrier can be held liable for an accident involving a stopped commercial vehicle if the driver fails to place warning markers next to a stopped vehicle, even if the vehicle has been stopped for less than 10 minutes, since regulations require the driver to place the signals as soon as possible.[448] A failure to place warning signs after remaining stopped in the roadway for more than 10 minutes may subject a carrier to punitive damages on the basis that the failure to comply with this guideline demonstrates a conscious indifference to public safety.[449] A driver can be held liable for stopping in an emergency lane on the shoulder of the roadway at night near lanes of high traffic because of the probability that his vehicle will not be seen by other drivers and the availability of safer resting spots.[450]

Practice Pointer: Determine if the tractor was equipped with emergency warning devices if the driver did not place them out before the accident.

M. Adverse Weather Conditions

A driver must exercise extreme caution when hazardous conditions, such as those caused by snow, ice, sleet, fog, mist, rain, dust or smoke, adversely affect visibility or traction.[451] Speed must be reduced when such conditions exist, and the operation of the vehicle must be discontinued if conditions become sufficiently dangerous.[452] When stopping a vehicle in adverse weather conditions endangers passengers, then the vehicle may be operated to the nearest point at which the safety of passengers is assured.[453] Federal regulations governing driving in adverse weather conditions set the standard of care for a commercial driver.[454] A driver who is involved in an accident during inclement weather is held to the standard of extreme care because of the regulations governing driving in adverse weather conditions.[455]

---

[442] 49 C.F.R. § 392.22(b)(2).
[443] 49 C.F.R. § 392.24.
[444] 49 C.F.R. § 392.25.
[445] Wood v. CRT Expedited, Inc., 419 P.2d 503 (Wy 2018).
[446] Sandberg Trucking, Inc. v. Johnson, 76 N.E.3d 178 (Ind. 2017).
[447] Bogdanski v. Budzik, 408 P.3d 1156 (Wy. 2018); Kimberlin v. PM Transport, Inc., 563 S.E.2d 665 (Va. 2002); Hageman v. TSI, Inc., 786 P.2d 452 (Col. 1989); Brandes v. Burbank, 613 F.3d 658 (7th Cir. 1980); Bruno v. Jackson, 2005 WL 1240979 (M.D. Pa.).
[448] Johnson v. Gmeinder, 2000 WL 246585 (D.Kan. 2000); Wallace v. Ener, 521 F.2d 215 (5th Cir. 1975).
[449] Fowler v. Smith, 516 S.E.2d 845 (Ga. 1999); Alfonso v. Robinson, 514 S.E.2d 615 (Va. 1999); Courtney v. Ivanov, 41 F.Supp.3d 453 (W.D.Penn. 2014).
[450] Heatherly v. Alexander, 421 F.3d 638 (8th Cir. 2005).
[451] 49 C.F.R. § 392.14.
[452] 49 C.F.R. § 392.14.
[453] 49 C.F.R. § 392.14.
[454] Weaver v. Chavez, 35 Cal. Rptr. 514 (2005).
[455] Crooks v. Sammons Trucking, Inc., 2001 WL 1654590 (Cal. 2001); Kimberlin v. PM Transport, Inc., 563 S.E.2d 665 (Va. 2002); Fisher v. Swift Transportation Co., Inc., 181 P.3d 601 (Mt. 2008).

Practice Pointer: A strong argument can be made that a commercial driver must use extreme care rather than ordinary care when driving in adverse weather conditions based on the federal regulations.

N. Texting While Driving & Cellphone Use

Texting includes entering or reading text from an electronic device but does not include entering or retrieving a telephone number or inputting or reading information into a navigation system.[456] Electronic devices include cellphones, pagers, computers or any other device used to input, write, send, receive or read text.[457] Truck drivers are prohibited from texting while driving which includes any time that the motor is running if the vehicle is in the roadway.[458] Texting is defined as any "electronic text retrieval or entry, short message service, emailing, instant messaging, accessing the internet, or pressing more than a single button to make a or receive a call."[459] Motor carriers cannot allow or require its drivers to engage in texting while driving.[460] Regulations also require a truck driver to use a hands-free cellphone while driving.[461]

Practice Pointer: Always request the cellphone records for both personal and business phones used by the truck driver.

O. Passengers in Tractor-Trailer

Unless specifically authorized in writing by the motor carrier, no driver shall transport any person or permit any person to be transported on any commercial vehicle other than a bus.[462] No written authorization shall be necessary for the transportation of employees or other persons assigned to a vehicle by the motor carrier, any person transported when aid is being rendered in case of an accident or emergency, or an attendant delegated to care for livestock.[463] The driver must make sure that the passenger is using the seat belt at all times that the vehicle is being operated on the public roadway.[464] A carrier cannot be held liable for an accident based solely an the presence of an unauthorized passenger in a tractor-trailer absent evidence that the passenger caused the accident.[465]

Practice Pointer: An unauthorized passenger can distract a driver causing an accident and may also void insurance coverage.

P. Crossing Railroad Tracks

A driver may not shift gears while crossing railroad tracks.[466] A driver must stop within 50 feet and not closer than 15 feet from a railroad crossing and listen and look for an oncoming train before crossing the tracks if he is operating (1) a bus transporting passengers, (2) a commercial vehicle transporting flammable, explosive or poisonous materials, (3) a cargo tank motor vehicle, whether loaded or empty, used for the transportation of any hazardous material, or (4) a cargo tank motor vehicle loaded with an exempt commodity or a commodity which has a temperature above its flashpoint at the time of loading.[467] A stop is not necessary at a streetcar crossing or railroad tracks used exclusively for switching purposes, at a railroad crossing when an officer or flagman directs traffic, at a crossing where a functioning traffic signal is transmitting a green light, at an abandoned

---

[456] 49 C.F.R. § 390.5.
[457] 49 C.F.R. § 390.5.
[458] 49 C.F.R. § 392.8.
[459] 49 C.F.R. § 390.5.
[460] 49 C.F.R. § 392.8(b).
[461] 49 C.F.R. § 392.82.
[462] 49 C.F.R. § 392.60(a).
[463] 49 C.F.R. § 392.60(a).
[464] 49 C.F.R. § 392.16.
[465] Fox v. Lyte, 143 A.D.2d 390 (N.Y. 1988).
[466] 49 C.F.R. § 392.10(a).
[467] 49 C.F.R. § 392.10(a).

railroad crossing, or at a spur line railroad grade crossing marked with a sign reading "Exempt."[468] In every other situation, a commercial vehicle approaching a railroad crossing must be driven at a rate of speed which will permit the vehicle to be stopped before reaching the nearest rail of such crossing and cannot be driven over such crossing until due caution has been taken to ascertain that the course is clear.[469]

Q. Hazardous Materials Transportation

Every motor vehicle transporting hazardous materials must be driven and parked in compliance with the laws, ordinances, and regulations of the State or jurisdiction in which it is being operated unless the Department of Transportation requires a more stringent obligation or restraint.[470] A vehicle transporting hazardous materials of any kind cannot be operated near an open fire unless the driver has first taken precautions to ascertain that the vehicle can pass safely without stopping [471] A vehicle transporting hazardous materials cannot be parked within 300 feet of an open fire.[472] No person may smoke or carry a lighted cigarette within 25 feet of a motor vehicle containing flammable or explosive materials.[473] When a vehicle transporting hazardous materials is being fueled, its engine must be turned off and a person must be in control of the fueling process while the fuel tank is filled.[474]

A driver transporting hazardous materials must examine the tires at the beginning of the trip and each time the vehicle is parked.[475] If a tire is flat, leaking or improperly inflated, the driver must cause the tire to be repaired, replaced or properly inflated before the vehicle is driven, except the vehicle may be driven to the nearest safe place.[476] If a tire is found to be overheated, the driver shall immediately remove the overheated tire and discontinue operation of the vehicle until the cause of the overheating is corrected.[477]

A motor carrier that transports hazardous materials must provide its drivers with instructions concerning the federal regulations governing hazardous materials and procedures to be followed in the event of an accident or delay.[478] States may designate certain routes for the transportation of non-radioactive hazardous material (NRHM)[479] and carriers shall comply with the State designations in transporting NRHM loads.[480]

A vehicle transporting explosive hazardous material must be attended by its driver or a qualified representative at all times unless the vehicle is located on the property of the carrier, shipper or consignee.[481] The vehicle may not be parked (1) within 5 feet of a traveled portion of a public street or highway, (2) on private property without the knowledge and consent of the person in charge of the property and who is aware of the hazardous nature of the materials, or (3) within 300 feet of a bridge, tunnel, dwelling or place where people work, congregate or assemble except for brief periods when the necessities of operation require the vehicle to be parked in such a manner.[482]

A vehicle containing hazardous materials other than explosive materials must be attended by its driver while located on a public street, highway or shoulder of a public highway.[483] The motor vehicle is considered to be attended if the person in charge of the vehicle is awake on the vehicle or within

---

[468] 49 C.F.R. § 392.10(b).
[469] 49 C.F.R. § 392.11.
[470] 49 C.F.R. § 397.3.
[471] 49 C.F.R. § 397.11.
[472] 49 C.F.R. § 397.11.
[473] 49 C.F.R. § 397.13.
[474] 49 C.F.R. § 397.15.
[475] 49 C.F.R. § 397.17(a).
[476] 49 C.F.R. § 397.17(b).
[477] 49 C.F.R. § 397.17(c).
[478] 49 C.F.R. § 397.19.
[479] 49 C.F.R. § 397.71.
[480] 49 C.F.R. § 397.67.
[481] 49 C.F.R. § 397.5(a) & (b).
[482] 49 C.F.R. § 397.7(a).
[483] 49 C.F.R. § 397.5(c).

100 feet of the vehicle with an unobstructed view.[484] The vehicle cannot be parked within 5 feet of the travel portion of a public street or highway except for brief periods when the necessities of operation require the vehicle to be parked in such a manner.[485]

R. Intermodal Equipment

On June 17, 2009, the FMCSA passed the first rules and regulations governing Intermodal Equipment Providers ("IEP") and operators. IEPs are now required to register with the FMCSA.[486] Intermodal equipment must be marked with the USDOT # of the IEP.[487] The FMCSA does not assign a safety rating to the IEP but does conduct roadability reviews of equipment and can take intermodal equipment out-of-service based on these reviews.[488] IEPs are subject to all the provisions of the FMCSR except the accident registers.[489] The IEP must systematically inspect, repair and maintain its intermodal equipment intended for interchange with a motor carrier and is responsible for conducting periodic inspections on all intermodal equipment.[490] The IEP must know and be familiar with all the safety regulations governing its equipment.[491] Truck drivers operating intermodal equipment must inspect the equipment before operating it on the roadway.[492] The truck driver must turn in a daily inspection report of the intermodal equipment to the IEP who must collect and maintain the reports.[493]

S. Buses

Every bus shall have a 2 inch wide line drawn at the rear of the driver's seat indicating that passengers may not occupy a space forward of the line.[494] A sign shall be posted near the front of the bus stating that it is a violation of the Federal Highway Administration's regulations for a bus to be operated with persons occupying the prohibited area.[495] Buses may not have any seat that is not securely fastened to the vehicle.[496] A bus may not be operated unless (1) all standees are rearward of the standee line, (2) all aisle seats conform to federal requirements, and (3) baggage and freight on the bus is stowed and secured in a manner which assures unrestricted freedom of movement to the driver and his proper operation of the bus, unobstructed access to all exits by any occupant of the bus, and protection of occupants of the bus against injury resulting from the falling or displacement of articles transported in the bus.[497]

Buses are required to have push-out windows or emergency exits.[498] Emergency exits on a bus must be clearly marked with the words "Emergency Door" or "Emergency Exit" and operating instructions on how to open the door.[499] These provisions do not apply to the transportation of prisoners.[500]

---

[484] 49 C.F.R. § 397.5(d).
[485] 49 C.F.R. § 397.7(b).
[486] 49 C.F.R. § 390.19.
[487] 49 C.F.R. § 390.21.
[488] 49 C.F.R. § 385.503.
[489] 49 C.F.R. § 390.3(h).
[490] 49 C.F.R. § 396.17
[491] 49 C.F.R. § 393.1.
[492] 49 C.F.R. § 392.7.
[493] 49 C.F.R. § 396.11(a)(2).
[494] 49 C.F.R. § 393.90.
[495] 49 C.F.R. § 393.90.
[496] 49 C.F.R. § 393.91.
[497] 49 C.F.R. § 392.62.
[498] 49 C.F.R. § 393.62.
[499] 49 C.F.R. § 393.62(e).
[500] 49 C.F.R. § 393.62(f).

T. Lights, Reflectors & Retroreflective Sheeting

Headlights must be capable of steady burning at all times.[501] All lighting devices required on vehicles must be capable of being operated at all times.[502] Guidelines for the color and positioning of lights on commercial vehicle are located in 49 C.F.R. § 393.11. Lights and reflectors on the vehicle must meet visibility requirements under nighttime conditions.[503] Reflectors must be applied to the side and rear of the trailer.[504] The required lamps and reflectors may not be obscured by the tailboard, by any part of the load, by dirt or otherwise.[505]

Retroreflective sheeting must be applied to each side of a trailer from as close to the front and rear as practicable.[506] The rear of each trailer must be equipped with retroreflective sheeting across the full width of the trailer and must have two pairs of white strips at the top corners of the trailer.[507] Every vehicle must be equipped with a hazard warning signal that will cause all turn signals to flash simultaneously as a hazard warning when necessary.[508] The wiring for the electrical system must comply with all applicable engineering standards.[509] If a claimant collides with the rear of a trailer in nighttime conditions, then the carrier can be held liable if the reflectors and lights are not operating properly or if there is no retroreflective sheeting on the trailer.[510]

Retroreflective Taping

Retroreflective taping is supposed to reflect headlights to warn approaching motorists of the trailer in the roadway.

**Practice Pointer: Retain a conspicuity expert to demonstrate the problems caused by lack of reflectors on a trailer.

---

[501] 49 C.F.R. § 393.24.
[502] 49 C.F.R. § 393.9.
[503] 49 C.F.R. § 393.25.
[504] 49 C.F.R. § 393.13(d).
[505] 49 C.F.R. § 392.33 & 393.9(b).
[506] 49 C.F.R. § 393.13(c).
[507] 49 C.F.R. § 393.13(c)(2)-(3).
[508] 49 C.F.R. § 393.19.
[509] 49 C.F.R. § 393.28.
[510] Quay v. Crawford, 788 So.2d 76 (Miss. 2001).

U. Brakes

A commercial vehicle or combination of vehicles must have brakes adequate to control the movements of the vehicle or combination of vehicles and to stop and hold the vehicle.[511] Each vehicle must meet applicable service, parking and emergency brake system requirements.[512] Every commercial vehicle, except an agricultural commodity trailer or pulpwood trailer, must be equipped with a parking brake system adequate to hold the vehicle under any condition of loading.[513] The driver of an agricultural commodity trailer or pulpwood trailer must carry chocking blocks sufficient to prevent movement when the trailer is parked.[514] Every commercial vehicle must have brakes on all wheels[515] and have an emergency braking system sufficient to stop a breakaway trailer independent of brake air, hydraulics and other pressure and controls.[516]

Brake tubing and hosing must be installed in such a manner that insures proper and continued function of the tubing or hosing and must be secured against chafing, kinking, or other mechanical damage.[517] All connections for air, vacuum or hydraulic braking must be secure and free of leaks, constrictions or other defects.[518] Brake lining must be installed on the brakes in such a manner as to prevent fading and grabbing and must be of adequate thickness to provide safe and reliable stopping of the vehicle.[519] The pushrod travel cannot exceed 80% of the rated stroke listed by the chamber manufacturer.[520] The reservoirs in the braking system must maintain adequate air pressure.[521] All brakes must be capable of operating at all times.[522] A vehicle must be equipped with a pressure gauge for the brake system, and a signal that provides a warning to the driver when a failure occurs in the vehicle's service brake system.[523] Automatic adjusting brakes are required to have an out-of-adjustment indicator light which activates if the brakes are out of adjustment.[524] The service brakes must be capable of generating a percentage of braking force and stopping distance in relation to the weight of the vehicle.[525]

A carrier can be held liable for an accident which occurs because a vehicle's brakes have not been properly maintained[526] or because the brakes do not meet the minimum braking force requirements.[527] A carrier can be held liable for punitive damages if the driver fails to conduct a pre-trip inspection and as a result fails to discover and correct problems with the vehicle's brakes.[528] A maintenance facility cannot be held liable for negligent maintenance of a vehicle's brakes if the driver fails to conduct the necessary pre-trip inspection to determine the condition of the brakes prior to the vehicle's operation and the driver operates the vehicle despite the brakes feeling funny.[529]

Practice Pointer: Trailer brakes are usually manually adjusted, and the slack adjusters are often outside of federal minimum limits. Retain a trucking expert to inspect the unit to determine if the brakes are properly adjusted.

---

[511] 49 C.F.R. § 393.40(a).
[512] 49 C.F.R. § 393.40(a).
[513] 49 C.F.R. § 393.41(a).
[514] 49 C.F.R. § 393.41(a).
[515] 49 C.F.R. § 393.42.
[516] 49 C.F.R. § 393.43.
[517] 49 C.F.R. § 393.45.
[518] 49 C.F.R. § 393.45(d).
[519] 49 C.F.R. § 393.47.
[520] 49 C.F.R. § 393.47(e).
[521] 49 C.F.R. § 393.50.
[522] 49 C.F.R. § 393.48(a).
[523] 49 C.F.R. § 393.51(a).
[524] 49 C.F.R. § 393.53.
[525] 49 C.F.R. § 393.52.
[526] Brannan v. Nevada Rock & Sand Co., 823 P.2d 291 (Nev. 1992).
[527] Schmidt v. Royer, 574 N.W.2d 618 (S.D. 1998).
[528] Burrows v. Core-Mark International, Inc., 54 F.3d 785 (9th Cir. 1995).
[529] Id.

V. Rear Guards

Every trailer must have a rear impact guard to protect against a vehicle going under the trailer during a rear impact collision with the exception of pole trailers, pulpwood trailers, low-chassis vehicles, special purpose vehicles and wheels back vehicles.[530] For trailers manufactured after January 26, 1998, the outermost surfaces of the horizontal member of the guard must extend within 4 inches of the side extremities of the trailer,[531] and the bottom edge of the guard must be less than 22 inches from the ground[532] with the guard itself within 12 inches of the rear extremity of the trailer.[533] For trailers manufactured after December 31, 1952, the guard must be within 18 inches of the side extremities of the trailer, 30 inches from the ground, and within 24 inches of the rear extremity of the trailer.[534] The rear impact guard must be substantially constructed and attached by means of bolts, welding, or other comparable means.[535] If the rear impact guard breaks in a rear-end collision, then the carrier can be held liable for improper welding and attachment of the guard and aggravation of the claimant's injuries resulting from the vehicle going under the trailer.[536]

Rear Guard

The rear guard is designed to keep a vehicle from traveling under the trailer in a rear end collision.

Although the FMCSR only apply to carriers, a manufacturer can also be held liable for a trailer that fails to meet federal guidelines requiring rear guards since this failure is evidence that a jury can consider in determining if the trailer is a defective product.[537] Federal regulations require a rear bumper or guard designed to provide protection during rear-end collisions with the trailer, and a trailer without a bumper or guard does not comply with this provision even though the trailer is less than the minimum height from the ground.[538] A manufacturer can be held liable for a defective rear guard, even if it conforms to minimum federal standards, if the claimant can prove that the industry

---

[530] 49 C.F.R. § 393.86.
[531] 49 C.F.R. § 393.86(a)(2).
[532] 49 C.F.R. § 393.86(a)(3).
[533] 49 C.F.R. § 393.86(a)(4).
[534] 49 C.F.R. § 393.86(b)(1).
[535] 49 C.F.R. § 393.86(b)(2).
[536] Quay v. Crawford, 788 So.2d 76 (Miss. 2001).
[537] Hagan v. Gemstate Manufacturing, Inc., 982 P.2d 1108 (Or. 1998).
[538] Id.

standard required stricter guidelines than the federal rules or that the guard was still unreasonably dangerous despite compliance with the federal guidelines.[539]

Practice Pointer: If the accident involves crush damage from riding under the rear of a trailer, consider a cause of action based on a defective rear guard. Preserve the rear guard, if present, and consider filing an action against both the trucking company and manufacturer.

W. Windows & Mirrors

Windows and windshields may be tinted as long as the tinted glazing is not less than 70 percent of the light at normal incidence.[540] No device may be mounted on the windshield lower than 6 inches below the upper edge of the windshield.[541] Decals must be placed within 4 inches of the bottom of the windshield.[542]

Every commercial vehicle must be equipped with a windshield wiping system with at least two windshield wiper blades.[543] The vehicle must be equipped with a method to remove ice, snow or frost on the outside of the windshield and condensation on the inside of the windshield from the driver's view.[544] Every vehicle must be equipped with two rear-vision mirrors, one at each side, firmly attached to the outside of the vehicle, and the mirrors must reflect to the driver a view of the highway to the rear and along both sides of the vehicle.[545]

X. Fuel Systems

Liquid fuel tanks must comply with construction guidelines and meet pressure and performance requirements.[546] The fuel system must be located within the width of the motor vehicle, and the fuel line must be flexible and secured against chafing, kinking or other causes of mechanical damage.[547] No driver or employee of a motor carrier may smoke or use an open flame in the vicinity of a motor vehicle being fueled or fuel a vehicle with the engine running, except when necessary.[548] When fueling a vehicle, the nozzle of the fuel hose must be in continuous contact with the intake pipe of the fuel tank, and the driver may not permit any person to engage in such activities as would be likely to result in fire or explosion.[549] No person shall dispatch or drive a commercial vehicle where an occupant has been affected by carbon monoxide, where carbon monoxide has been detected in the interior of the vehicle, or when a mechanical condition of the vehicle is discovered which would be likely to produce a hazard to the occupants by reason of carbon monoxide.[550]

Y. Frames, Axles & Steering Systems

The frame of any commercial vehicle cannot be cracked, loose, sagging or broken.[551] Bolts or brackets securing the cab or the body of the vehicle to the frame cannot be loose, broken or missing.[552] The cab compartment doors or door parts used as an entrance or exit cannot be missing or broken or wired shut.[553] The hood must be securely fastened and the front bumper cannot be missing, loosely

---

[539] Detillier v. Sullivan, 714 So.2d 244 (La. 1998); Rapp v. Singh, 152 F.Supp.2d 694 (E.D. Pa. 2001); Garcia v. Rivera, 160 A.D.2d 274 (N.Y. 1990).
[540] 49 C.F.R. § 393.60(d).
[541] 49 C.F.R. § 393.60(e)(1).
[542] 49 C.F.R. § 393.60(e)(2).
[543] 49 C.F.R. § 393.78(a).
[544] 49 C.F.R. § 393.79.
[545] 49 C.F.R. § 393.80(a).
[546] 49 C.F.R. § 393.67.
[547] 49 C.F.R. § 393.65.
[548] 49 C.F.R. § 392.50.
[549] 49 C.F.R. § 392.50.
[550] 49 C.F.R. § 392.66(a).
[551] 49 C.F.R. § 393.201(a).
[552] 49 C.F.R. § 393.201(b).
[553] 49 C.F.R. § 393.203(a).

attached or protruding beyond the confines of the vehicle so as to create a hazard.[554] Wheels and rims cannot be cracked or broken and no nuts or bolts may be missing or loose.[555] No axle positioning part can be cracked, broken, loose, missing or out of alignment.[556] Adjustable axle assemblies cannot have locking pins missing or disengaged and the leaf springs, coil springs and torsion bars cannot be cracked, broken, or out of position.[557] The air pressure regulator valve cannot allow air into the suspension system until at least 55 psi is in the braking system, and air leakage shall not be greater than 3 psi in a 5 minute time period when the air gauge shows normal pressure.[558] A carrier can be held liable for the rear axle separating from the chassis and striking another vehicle without proof of negligence since the separation of the axle would not have happened without the negligence of the driver in failing to properly maintain the chassis and axles.[559]

The steering wheel must be secured and cannot have any spokes cracked through or missing.[560] The steering column must be securely fastened and universal joints cannot be worn, faulty or repaired by welding.[561] All components of the power steering system must be in operating condition and have sufficient fluid in the reservoir.[562]

Z. Towing Devices

Coupling devices connecting vehicles must be designed, constructed, and installed so that when the combination is operated in a straight line the path of the towed vehicle will not deviate more than 3 inches to either side of the path of the vehicle that tows it.[563] The fifth wheel is the device on the back of the tractor that locks onto the kingpin on the trailer to connect the tractor to the trailer. Every fifth wheel must have a locking mechanism to prevent separation of the upper and lower half of the fifth wheel assembly.[564] A trailer must be connected with a tow-bar that is structurally adequate for the weight being drawn and is properly and securely mounted with a locking device that prevents accidental separation of the trailer.[565] A trailer must be connected to the towing vehicle by a safety device to prevent the trailer from breaking loose in the event the tow-bar fails or is disconnected.[566]

Practice Pointer: If the accident involves detachment of a trailer, consider a cause of action based on a defective tow bar. Remember to preserve the tow bar, if present, and consider filing an action against both the trucking company and manufacturer.

AA. Tires

No commercial motor vehicle may be operated on any tire that (1) has body ply or belt material exposed through the tread or sidewall, (2) has any tread or sidewall separation, (3) is flat or has an audible leak, or (4) has a cut to the extent that the ply or belt material is exposed.[567] Any tire on the front wheels of a bus, truck, or truck tractor must have a tread groove pattern depth of at least 4/32 of an inch at any point in a major tread groove.[568] All other tires must have a tread groove pattern

---

[554] 49 C.F.R. § 393.203(c) & (e).
[555] 49 C.F.R. § 393.205.
[556] 49 C.F.R. § 393.207(a).
[557] 49 C.F.R. § 393.207(b)-(e).
[558] 49 C.F.R. § 393.207(f).
[559] Gautreaux v. W.W. Rowland Trucking Co., Inc., 757 So.2d 87 (La. 2000).
[560] 49 C.F.R. § 393.209(a).
[561] 49 C.F.R. § 393.209(c) & (d).
[562] 49 C.F.R. § 393.209(e).
[563] 49 C.F.R. § 393.70(a).
[564] 49 C.F.R. § 393.70(b).
[565] 49 C.F.R. § 393.70(c).
[566] 49 C.F.R. § 393.70(d).
[567] 49 C.F.R. § 393.75(a).
[568] 49 C.F.R. § 393.75(b).

depth of at least 2/32 of an inch when measured in a major tread groove.[569] Motor vehicles cannot be operated with loads that exceed a weight greater than the tire's capacity.[570]

Practice Pointer: In dry weather, tires with less tread depth actually stop a vehicle faster than tires with more tread depth. The lack of tread depth is only a factor in an accident involving wet conditions.

BB. Speedometer & Radar Detectors

Every vehicle must be equipped with a speedometer indicating vehicle speed in miles per hour and operating within 5 mph of the actual speed.[571] A carrier can be held liable for its failure to have an operating speedometer in a vehicle if speed is a contributing factor in the collision.[572] No driver shall use a radar detector in a commercial vehicle or operate a commercial vehicle that is equipped with or contains any radar detector.[573] No motor carrier shall allow a driver to operate a motor vehicle that is equipped with a radar detector.[574]

Practice Pointer: The use of a radar device is strictly forbidden by the federal regulations and provides an aggravating circumstance that usually allows the imposition of punitive damages.

CC. Miscellaneous Equipment & Accessories

A sleeper berth must be equipped with a means of preventing ejection of the occupant of the sleeper berth during deceleration of the vehicle.[575] Every vehicle must be equipped with a horn in such a condition as to give an adequate and reliable warning signal.[576] Any exhaust system must be designed where its location will not result in burning, charring or damaging the electrical wiring, the fuel supply, or any combustible part of the motor vehicle.[577] The flooring of all vehicles must be substantially constructed so as to be free of unnecessary holes and openings to minimize the entrance of fumes, exhaust gases or fire.[578]

Any television viewer or screen must be placed in the vehicle in such a position that it is not visible to the driver while he is operating the vehicle and cannot be operated by the driver from his seat.[579] The noise level within the interior of the vehicle cannot exceed 90 decibels.[580] Every power unit must be equipped with a fire extinguisher that is properly filled and located so that it is readily accessible for use.[581] Each commercial vehicle must be equipped with a seatbelt.[582] A driver must be properly restrained with a seat belt when operating a commercial vehicle.[583] No open flame heater may be used while the vehicle is in motion.[584] Every motor vehicle must be properly lubricated and free of oil and grease leaks.[585]

---

[569] 49 C.F.R. § 393.75(c).
[570] 49 C.F.R. § 393.75(f).
[571] 49 C.F.R. § 393.82.
[572] Greist v. Phillips, 906 P.2d 789 (Or. 1995).
[573] 49 C.F.R. § 392.71(a).
[574] 49 C.F.R. § 392.71(b).
[575] 49 C.F.R. § 393.76(h).
[576] 49 C.F.R. § 393.81.
[577] 49 C.F.R. § 393.83(a).
[578] 49 C.F.R. § 393.84.
[579] 49 C.F.R. § 393.88.
[580] 49 C.F.R. § 393.94(b).
[581] 49 C.F.R. § 393.95(a).
[582] 49 C.F.R. § 393.93.
[583] 49 C.F.R. § 392.16.
[584] 49 C.F.R. § 392.67.
[585] 49 C.F.R. § 396.5.

VIII. Electronic Control Module

Commercial truck tractors have an Electronic Control Module ("ECM") responsible for monitoring and controlling important engine and vehicle parameters. The ECM is sometimes referred to as the "black box" for the truck and records data concerning the vehicle's operation including speed, braking, use of clutch and use of cruise control. The type and amount of data recorded by the ECM varies according to engine manufacturer. The data can be downloaded with the right type of software.

The ECM may record data generally over a daily or monthly activity period and also when the tractor-trailer rapidly decelerates at a rate that exceeds a pre-set threshold. The threshold usually is met during a "hard braking event" but can also occur during a collision if the impact slows the truck down significantly. As part of a hard braking event, the ECM may record vehicle speed, clutch and brake status and throttle position. Certain ECMs will also record a "last stop" event whenever the engine is turned off. The ECM "last stop" data will be overwritten if the vehicle is placed back into service, and "hard braking event" data will be overwritten if the vehicle is placed back into operation and another hard braking event occurs. Because of the possibility that the data will be lost, it is extremely important to download any available data from the ECM as soon as possible after an incident.

A. Daily and Periodic Engine Usage Data from the ECM

The ECM may record the vehicle's speed on a daily basis.

DDEC® Reports – Daily Engine Usage

Print Date: Nov 12, 2007 01:41 PM (EST)

Southeast Collision
2005 Commercial Dr
Brunswick, Ga 31525
912-267-6900

Date Range: 11/11/2008 to 09/12/2008 (CST)
Vehicle ID: 8687
Driver ID:

Date:	11/04/2008		Total (hh:mm)	13:41	05:40	04:39
Start Time:	02:33:52 (CST)		Hour (CST)	Drive (min)	Idle (min)	Off (min)
			00:00-02:00	0	0	120
Odometer:	956324.0 mi		02:00-04:00	69	17	34
			04:00-06:00	54	66	0
Distance:	772.4 mi		06:00-08:00	99	21	0
Fuel:	122.25 gal		08:00-10:00	26	94	0
			10:00-12:00	107	13	0
Fuel Economy:	6.32 mpg		12:00-14:00	104	16	0
			14:00-16:00	48	72	0
Average Speed:	56.4 mph		16:00-18:00	92	28	0
			18:00-20:00	112	8	0
			20:00-22:00	110	5	5
			22:00-24:00	0	0	120

Date:	11/03/2008		Total (hh:mm)	00:40	00:07	23:13
Start Time:	08:23:58 (CST)		Hour (CST)	Drive (min)	Idle (min)	Off (min)
			00:00-02:00	0	0	120
Odometer:	956292.2 mi		02:00-04:00	0	0	120
			04:00-06:00	0	0	120
Distance:	31.8 mi		06:00-08:00	0	0	120
Fuel:	4.00 gal		08:00-10:00	40	7	73
			10:00-12:00	0	0	120
Fuel Economy:	7.95 mpg		12:00-14:00	0	0	120
			14:00-16:00	0	0	120
Average Speed:	47.7 mph		16:00-18:00	0	0	120
			18:00-20:00	0	0	120
			20:00-22:00	0	0	120
			22:00-24:00	0	0	120

Date:	10/31/2008		Total (hh:mm)	10:13	02:36	11:11
Start Time:	02:39:48 (CST)		Hour (CST)	Drive (min)	Idle (min)	Off (min)
			00:00-02:00	0	0	120
Odometer:	955683.3 mi		02:00-04:00	49	31	40
			04:00-06:00	69	51	0
Distance:	608.9 mi		06:00-08:00	105	15	0
Fuel:	100.75 gal		08:00-10:00	110	10	0
			10:00-12:00	75	45	0
Fuel Economy:	6.04 mpg		12:00-14:00	120	0	0
			14:00-16:00	85	4	31
Average Speed:	59.6 mph		16:00-18:00	0	0	120
			18:00-20:00	0	0	120
			20:00-22:00	0	0	120
			22:00-24:00	0	0	120

11127GAA.XTR   Engine S/N: 06R0441201   ECM S/W Version: 28.00   Version 6.2   Page 2

Grant vs Bennett Truck Transport   00076
Georgia State Patrol - SCRT No' 4-060-07

The ECM may also record the vehicle's speed over a given period of time such as on a quarterly basis.

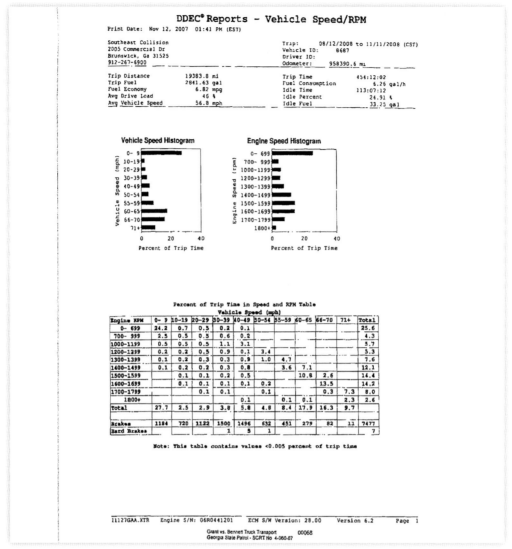

B. Hard Braking Event

We have included below a DDEC printout from the ECM of a Detroit Diesel Engine concerning a hard braking event.

DDEC® Reports - Hard Brake #1

Print Date: Nov 12, 2007 01:41 PM (EST)

Southeast Collision
2005 Commercial Dr
Brunswick, Ga 31525
912-267-6900

Trip: 08/12/2008 to 11/11/2008 (CST)
Vehicle ID: 8687
Driver ID:
Odometer: 958390.6 mi

Trip Distance	19383.8 mi	Trip Time	454:12:02
Trip Fuel	2841.63 gal	Fuel Consumption	6.26 gal/h
Fuel Economy	6.82 mpg	Idle Time	113:07:12
Avg Drive Load	46 %	Idle Percent	24.91 %
Avg Vehicle Speed	56.8 mph	Idle Fuel	33.25 gal

Incident Time: 11/04/2008 10:17:14 (CST)   Incident Odometer: 956558.4 mi

Time	Vehicle Speed (mph)	Engine Speed (rpm)	Brake	Clutch	Engine Load (%)	Throttle (%)	Cruise	Diagnostic Code
-1:00	45.5	1456	No	No	86.50	82.40	No	No
-0:59	45.5	1461	No	No	86.50	82.40	No	No
-0:58	45.5	1464	No	No	65.00	69.20	No	No
-0:57	45.5	1465	No	No	68.50	70.00	No	No
-0:56	45.5	1459	No	No	33.00	46.80	No	No
-0:55	45.5	1458	No	No	43.50	54.00	No	No
-0:54	45.5	1457	No	No	33.50	47.20	No	No
-0:53	45.5	1451	No	No	18.00	33.20	No	No
-0:52	45.0	1445	No	No	19.00	34.00	No	No
-0:51	45.0	1443	No	No	19.00	34.80	No	No
-0:50	45.0	1436	No	No	8.50	15.20	No	No
-0:49	44.5	1416	No	No	0.00	0.00	No	No
-0:48	44.0	1415	No	No	0.00	0.00	No	No
-0:47	44.0	1404	No	No	0.00	0.00	No	No
-0:46	44.0	1408	No	No	28.00	42.80	No	No
-0:45	44.0	1401	No	No	44.50	54.00	No	No
-0:44	44.0	1412	No	No	47.00	55.60	No	No
-0:43	44.5	1419	No	No	34.00	47.20	No	No
-0:42	44.0	1406	No	No	0.00	0.00	No	No
-0:41	43.5	1391	No	No	0.00	0.00	No	No
-0:40	43.0	1395	No	No	13.50	23.20	No	No
-0:39	43.0	1375	No	No	51.00	78.80	No	No
-0:38	43.0	1377	No	No	65.50	88.40	No	No
-0:37	43.5	1382	No	No	95.00	96.80	No	No
-0:36	43.5	1398	No	No	99.50	98.40	No	No
-0:35	44.0	1407	No	No	99.50	98.40	No	No
-0:34	44.5	1417	No	No	96.00	90.00	No	No
-0:33	44.5	1428	No	No	97.00	92.00	No	No
-0:32	45.0	1435	No	No	97.00	91.60	No	No
-0:31	45.0	1450	No	No	97.00	91.60	No	No
-0:30	45.5	1457	No	No	97.00	92.00	No	No
-0:29	45.5	1460	No	No	74.50	74.40	No	No
-0:28	45.5	1462	No	No	69.00	70.80	No	No
-0:27	45.5	1463	No	No	69.00	70.80	No	No
-0:26	45.5	1463	No	No	51.50	60.00	No	No
-0:25	45.5	1461	No	No	62.50	66.80	No	No
-0:24	45.5	1462	No	No	58.50	64.40	No	No
-0:23	46.0	1463	No	No	65.00	68.40	No	No
-0:22	46.0	1463	No	No	68.00	70.00	No	No
-0:21	46.0	1467	No	No	49.50	58.00	No	No

11127GAA.XTR   Engine S/N: 06R0441201   ECM S/W Version: 28.00   Version 6.2   Page 1

Grant vs Bennett Truck Transport
Georgia State Patrol - SCRT No· 4-060-07   00091

DDEC® Reports - Hard Brake #1

Print Date: Nov 12, 2007 01:41 PM (EST)

Southeast Collision
2005 Commercial Dr
Brunswick, Ga 31525
912-267-6900

Trip: 08/12/2008 to 11/11/2008 (CST)
Vehicle ID: 8687
Driver ID:
Odometer: 958390.6 mi

Incident Time: 11/04/2008 10:17:14 (CST)   Incident Odometer: 956558.4 mi

Time	Vehicle Speed (mph)	Engine Speed (rpm)	Brake	Clutch	Engine Load (%)	Throttle (%)	Cruise	Diagnostic Code
-0:20	45.5	1454	No	No	51.00	59.60	No	No
-0:19	45.5	1454	No	No	55.00	61.60	No	No
-0:18	45.5	1450	No	No	72.00	72.80	No	No
-0:17	45.5	1455	No	No	52.50	60.00	No	No
-0:16	45.5	1450	No	No	53.50	60.80	No	No
-0:15	45.5	1450	No	No	73.50	73.60	No	No
-0:14	45.5	1449	No	No	72.50	72.80	No	No
-0:13	45.0	1449	No	No	68.50	71.20	No	No
-0:12	45.0	1447	No	No	70.00	71.60	No	No
-0:11	45.0	1440	No	No	71.00	71.60	No	No
-0:10	44.5	1439	No	No	73.50	73.60	No	No
-0:09	44.5	1423	No	No	64.50	67.20	No	No
-0:08	44.5	1420	No	No	73.50	74.00	No	No
-0:07	44.5	1428	No	No	79.00	77.20	No	No
-0:06	44.5	1426	No	No	61.50	65.60	No	No
-0:05	45.0	1428	No	No	63.00	66.80	No	No
-0:04	45.0	1440	No	No	65.00	68.80	No	No
-0:03	45.5	1449	No	No	68.50	70.40	No	No
-0:02	45.5	1457	No	No	53.50	60.80	No	No
-0:01	42.5	1348	Yes	No	0.00	0.00	No	No
0:00	35.0	1111	Yes	No	0.00	0.00	No	No
+0:01	30.0	955	Yes	No	0.00	0.00	No	No
+0:02	23.5	760	Yes	No	0.00	0.00	No	No
+0:03	18.5	602	Yes	No	4.50	0.00	No	No
+0:04	12.5	617	Yes	Yes	2.00	0.00	No	No
+0:05	8.5	601	Yes	Yes	4.50	0.00	No	No
+0:06	7.0	647	No	Yes	87.00	42.00	No	No
+0:07	7.0	606	No	Yes	3.50	0.00	No	No
+0:08	6.5	985	No	Yes	0.00	0.00	No	No
+0:09	6.5	929	No	Yes	17.50	23.60	No	No
+0:10	8.0	698	No	Yes	46.00	20.00	No	No
+0:11	7.5	642	No	Yes	48.00	16.80	No	No
+0:12	7.5	1345	No	Yes	20.00	36.80	No	No
+0:13	8.0	1217	No	Yes	0.00	0.00	No	No
+0:14	7.5	1379	No	Yes	0.00	0.00	No	No

11127GAA.XTR   Engine S/N: 06R0441201   ECM S/W Version: 28.00   Version 6.2   Page 2

Grant vs Bennett Truck Transport
Georgia State Patrol - SCRT No 4-080-07   00092

The ZERO time is the point at which the ECM "woke up" as a result of the hard braking event. The ZERO time could correspond to the point of impact if the event that woke up the ECM was the impact itself, or it will be the point at which the truck driver began braking hard enough to exceed the minimum deceleration threshold, which could be either before or after the initial impact. The ECM goes back for a minute and records the data leading up to the hard braking event and continues to record data for several seconds after the hard braking event. In this case, the ECM has recorded a number of items, but most important for an accident reconstruction would be (1) the vehicle's speed; (2) whether the brake was engaged and (3) whether the cruise control was on.

C. Last Stop Event

The data from a last stop event is similar to the record of a hard braking event but the ZERO time is the point at which the vehicle came to a stop.

```
                    DDEC® Reports  -  Last Stop Record
Print Date:  Nov 12, 2007  01:41 PM (EST)

Southeast Collision                          Trip:      08/12/2008 to 11/11/2008 (CST)
2005 Commercial Dr                           Vehicle ID:      8687
Brunswick, Ga 31525                          Driver ID:
912-267-6900                                 Odometer:        958390.6 mi

Last Stop Time: 11/11/2008 05:57:01 (CST)    Last Stop Odometer: 958390.6 mi
```

Time	Vehicle Speed (mph)	Engine Speed (rpm)	Brake	Clutch	Engine Load (%)	Throttle (%)	Cruise	Diagnostic Code
-0:19	11.0	1179	No	Yes	0.00	0.00	No	No
-0:18	10.5	1144	No	Yes	6.00	8.00	No	No
-0:17	10.5	1128	No	Yes	3.50	4.80	No	No
-0:16	10.5	1083	No	Yes	4.00	5.20	No	No
-0:15	10.5	1093	No	Yes	3.50	4.40	No	No
-0:14	10.0	1072	No	Yes	2.00	2.40	No	No
-0:13	9.5	1006	No	Yes	0.00	0.00	No	No
-0:12	8.5	879	No	Yes	0.00	0.00	No	No
-0:11	8.0	832	No	Yes	1.00	0.80	No	No
-0:10	7.0	760	No	Yes	3.50	2.00	No	No
-0:09	7.0	729	No	Yes	10.00	5.20	No	No
-0:08	7.0	739	No	Yes	16.50	8.80	No	No
-0:07	6.0	644	No	Yes	0.00	0.00	No	No
-0:06	6.0	728	No	Yes	40.00	20.00	No	No
-0:05	6.5	698	No	Yes	24.50	10.80	No	No
-0:04	6.5	718	No	Yes	0.00	0.00	No	No
-0:03	6.5	602	Yes	Yes	4.00	0.00	No	No
-0:02	5.0	601	Yes	Yes	4.50	0.00	No	No
-0:01	4.0	601	Yes	Yes	4.50	0.00	No	No
0:00	3.0	601	Yes	Yes	5.00	0.00	No	No
+0:01	0.0	600	Yes	Yes	5.00	0.00	No	No
+0:02	0.0	600	Yes	Yes	4.50	0.00	No	No
+0:03	0.0	600	Yes	Yes	4.50	0.00	No	No
+0:04	0.0	600	Yes	Yes	4.50	0.00	No	No
+0:05	0.0	600	Yes	Yes	5.00	0.00	No	No
+0:06	0.0	600	Yes	Yes	4.50	0.00	No	No
+0:07	0.0	600	Yes	Yes	5.00	0.00	No	No
+0:08	0.0	600	Yes	Yes	5.00	0.00	No	No
+0:09	0.0	600	Yes	Yes	5.00	0.00	No	No
+0:10	0.0	600	No	Yes	5.00	0.00	No	No
+0:11	0.0	600	No	No	4.50	0.00	No	No
+0:12	0.0	600	No	No	4.50	0.00	No	No
+0:13	0.0	600	No	No	5.00	0.00	No	No
+0:14	0.0	600	No	No	5.00	0.00	No	No
+0:15	0.0	600	No	No	4.50	0.00	No	No

```
11127GAA.XTR   Engine S/N: 06R0441201    ECM S/W Version: 28.00    Version 6.2    Page 3
                      Grant vs Bennett Truck Transport      00089
                      Georgia State Patrol - SCRT No 4-060-07
```

D. Types of Engines

The type of engine will determine what data is kept in the ECM and can be downloaded. We have included below a list of the different types of engines and the likely information kept in the ECM of each engine.

1. Detroit Diesel: May have engine and systems configuration data, trip/event data recording, two hard brake events, one last stop event, engine usage history.
2. Mercedes-Benz: May have engine and systems configuration data, trip/event data recording, two hard brake events, one last stop event, engine usage history.
3. Cummins: May have engine and systems configuration data, trip/event data recording, three hard brake events.
4. Caterpillar: May have engine and systems configuration data, trip/event data recording, one hard brake event.
5. Mack: May have engine and systems configuration data, trip/event data recording, two hard brake events, engine usage history.
6. Volvo: May have engine and systems configuration data, trip/event data recording, two hard brake events, engine usage history.
7. International: May have engine and systems configuration data, trip/event data recording, two hard brake events, two last stop events.

Practice Pointer: Download the ECM data as soon as possible and have a certified accident reconstructionist analyze the data for relevant information.

IX. Computer Data & Systems

Trucking companies often have computer systems that utilize the information from the ECM and from GPS sensors placed into the vehicle to monitor the whereabouts of the vehicle and fuel consumption and have other features that record information.[586] There are also a variety of collision-avoidance computer systems that warn the driver when he is drifting outside of his lane of travel such as VORAD or warn the driver when he is approaching a vehicle at an unsafe closing speed. The tractor may be equipped with a computer messaging system such as Qualcomm or PeopleNet to relay messages about traffic and loads and to communicate with dispatch. These computer systems contain a significant amount of data that may be relevant to the trucking company's operations or the cause of the collision.

A. Messaging Systems

There are numerous types of messaging systems that are utilized by the trucking industry including PeopleNet, DriverTech, Teletrac, Dynafleet, Xdata, XataNet, MobileNet, FleetMatics. But the most popular messaging system is Qualcomm and so many times people generically refer to these systems as Qualcomm systems. The Qualcomm electronic messaging system allows the user to communicate with dispatch through messages similar to a text message or e-mail.

Qualcomm System

There is a computer screen and keyboard inside the cab of the tractor.

---

[586] Electronic Data Checklist, Trucking Checklists 3.

The messages are usually stored in the system for a period of 7 to 30 days and can be downloaded from the master server.

Qualcomm Messages

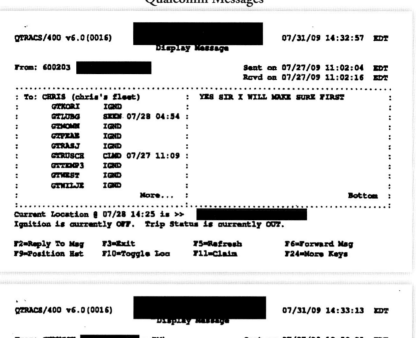

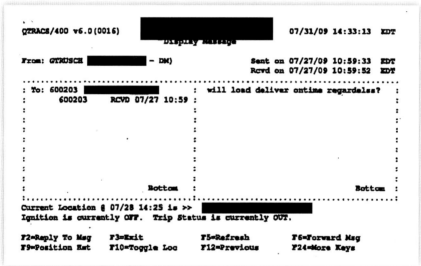

B. Load Information

The Qualcomm system tracks loads from pickup to delivery both for logistic purposes and for billing of the shipper.

```
Order # H718777 (?)     BOL # 43138964-60            Inv # 9395254 Status E
Shipper Code   25225    Load at Code 157545          Consignee Code  65760




                                                    GA                    TN
Div 005     Zip 80401   PU Area ATL Zip 30297   DL Area MEM Zip 38118
Bill to Code  25225     Orig FP GA ForestPark   Dest MEMPTN Memphis
                        Lds 01 Weight 0037774 PCS 87120 Eq Type V3 OM LIVE
                        P/U Apt N P/U 126 126 /  700 1400 Load N  P/L
                     CO Del Apt N Del 127 127 / 1500 1500 Unld N  L/D
                        JIT N HV N HZ   Trlr        EstRv  52088 POD 3 Rcv N
Zip 80401     Rail      ShpDt 0126 1400 Comm 0990 FREIGHT ALL KINDS
Plts 00 SL# 0136918            P/C C Temp    to    Miles  378 Load# 01
Ld Cont DAVE          Ph 404 3617585 Con Cont *         Ph 901 3752000
Loads Dispatched  01 PO # 4500254335         User JACKC    D/T 0122 1308


C# Type City    Name        Comment
001 C       65760         CAN DROP 16 HOURS PRIOR TO APPOINTMENT TIME
002 C       65760         NO SOONER!
003 O                     RELY# 43138964-08
004 C                     VOIDED DISP 01 ON 28477 BY PJB 01/26 10:15   +

ENTER Disp F2=Note F3=Exit F4=View Rte F15=Flgs  F7=S/O Inq F9=Frt F24=Mor Key
```

C. Driver Master

The Qualcomm system has a feature where each driver has a separate electronic file listing any comments about the driver's performance or safety issues.

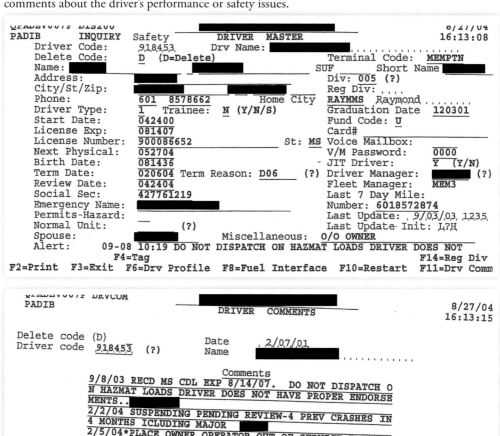

D. Tractor Master

The system creates an electronic file for each vehicle.

```
PADIB      INQUIRY                  UNIT MASTER                       8/27/04
                                                                     16:10:58
     Unit Code . . . . .   28477
     Delete/AVAS Code: .   D   (A/D)
     Owner Code  . . . .   XTAHA
     Fleet . . . . . . .   08 (01-99)        License Group Cd .
     License . . . . . .   2CK497            Driver Manager . .   ESLICK (?)
     Year Made . . . . .   2003              Fleet Manager  . .   PHX10
     Make  . . . . . . .   FREIGHTLINER      Division . . . . .   005  (?)
     Serial Number . . .                     Engine Code  . . .   D7
     Axles . . . . . . .   3
                                             Description  . . .   IELC
     Empty Weight  . . .   017400            Gross Weight . . .   080000
     Fuel Type . . . . .   D                 City Truck . . . .   N
     Cost New  . . . . .       83500         Insurance Amt  . .
     Date in Service . .   031803            Term Date  . . . .   060704
     Base State Code . .   OK                Terminal . . . . .   PHOEAZ
     Cost Center . . . .   996  Finance: _   Last Upd dt  6/07/04 Tm 0535 Init RHE
     Pay Type  . . . . .   M                 Matrix: Stop  PickUp Load Empty Pct%
     AVAS Customer Code               Empty Loaded
     Unit Pay Percent  .   00000     0820     0820           MPG: Low    High
     Unit Type Code  . .   3X                                     0400    0750
     NY TMT  . . . . . .   412308            Ohio HUT . . . . .
F3=Exit   F4=Owner Upd   F6=Hub Info   F8=Fuel  F10=Restart  F11=Comment
```

```
PADIB                          Tractor Comments                        8/27/04
                                                                      16:11:08

Delete code (D)    _        Tractor Code   28477       Date    3/18/03

                                 Comments
           3/18/03 TYPED 45 DAY TEMP(TP457820)ISSD '03 IFTA S
           TKRS GAVE BOOK TO O/O DIV -HM
                     TEMP EXP 5/01/03
           3/19/03 ORD WHITE CO VIN#S -HM
           3/24/03 ORD TX INTRA ******************HM
           4/8/03 SENT CO VIN#S TO MEM ATT:              *****
           4/21/03 OK PLT IN PHX    SP
           4/21/03 DUP REG IN FILE  SP
           4/22/03 @ 12:55PM DORA FROM MEMPHIS REQ PLT/REG TO
             GO TO

           5/27/03 REFAXED REQ FOR TX INTRA (STILL HASNT COME
             IN ) ************* HM                                       +

F3=Exit, F5=Update, F10-Restart
```

E. GPS Tracking

As part of most messaging systems, the tractor and /or trailer is monitored with a GPS system that tracks the location of the vehicle. The system will "ping" the vehicle on a regular basis, usually every hour, and record the location of the vehicle at that time. The system will also record the location of the vehicle whenever a message is sent or received over the electronic messaging system.

XataNet Vehicle Trip Report

From:	Mon 06/27/11 12:00a ET		Organization:	Spartanburg	
Through:	Wed 06/29/11 11:59p ET		Vehicle:	4811	

Motion Event	Location	Date/Time	Miles	Avg MPH	MPG
Motion Start	PILOT - GAFFNEY, SC	06/27/11 04:32p			
	PILOT - GAFFNEY, SC	06/27/11 04:33p	0.1	6.0	
	2.6 mi W of Gaffney, SC	06/27/11 04:34p	0.1	6.0	
	3.0 mi W of Gaffney, SC	06/27/11 04:35p	0.7	42.0	2.8
	2.7 mi N of Cowpens, SC	06/27/11 04:41p	5.0	50.0	3.6
	4.0 mi E of Valley Falls, SC	06/27/11 04:47p	7.2	72.0	4.4
	2.8 mi E of Valley Falls, SC	06/27/11 04:48p	1.2	72.0	3.2
	0.3 mi W of Valley Falls, SC	06/27/11 04:51p	3.1	62.0	5.0
	1.0 mi W of Southern Shops, SC	06/27/11 04:53p	2.9	87.0	3.9
	2.2 mi W of Southern Shops, SC	06/27/11 04:54p	1.3	78.0	5.2
	1.6 mi E of Wellford, SC	06/27/11 04:57p	2.9	58.0	5.8
	1.5 mi E of Startex, SC	06/27/11 04:58p	0.8	48.0	6.4
	1.8 mi E of Startex, SC	06/27/11 05:00p	0.6	18.0	2.4
	TF yard 3 SPARTANBURG - Spartanburg, SC	06/27/11 05:01p	0.4	24.0	3.2
	TF yard 3 SPARTANBURG - Spartanburg, SC	06/27/11 05:03p	0.2	6.0	
Motion Stop	TF yard 3 SPARTANBURG - Spartanburg, SC	06/27/11 05:03p	0.1		
			26.6	51.5	4.3

The system can also record speeds using the GPS technology.

XataNet Second by Second Report

XATAScope Second by Second Report

From: Tue 06/28/11 01:15a ET
Through: Tue 06/28/11 02:00a ET

Organization: Spartanburg
Vehicle: 4811

Date / Time	MPH	Date / Time	MPH
06/28/11 01:15:00a	46	06/28/11 01:15:30a	29
06/28/11 01:15:01a	46	06/28/11 01:15:31a	32
06/28/11 01:15:02a	46	06/28/11 01:15:32a	32
06/28/11 01:15:03a	43	06/28/11 01:15:33a	32
06/28/11 01:15:04a	43	06/28/11 01:15:34a	32
06/28/11 01:15:05a	43	06/28/11 01:15:35a	35
06/28/11 01:15:06a	43	06/28/11 01:15:36a	35
06/28/11 01:15:07a	43	06/28/11 01:15:37a	35
06/28/11 01:15:08a	43	06/28/11 01:15:38a	35
06/28/11 01:15:09a	43	06/28/11 01:15:39a	38
06/28/11 01:15:10a	43	06/28/11 01:15:40a	38
06/28/11 01:15:11a	43	06/28/11 01:15:41a	38
06/28/11 01:15:12a	43	06/28/11 01:15:42a	38
06/28/11 01:15:13a	43	06/28/11 01:15:43a	38
06/28/11 01:15:14a	43	06/28/11 01:15:44a	41
06/28/11 01:15:15a	43	06/28/11 01:15:45a	41
06/28/11 01:15:16a	43	06/28/11 01:15:46a	41
06/28/11 01:15:17a	39	06/28/11 01:15:47a	41
06/28/11 01:15:18a	39	06/28/11 01:15:48a	41
06/28/11 01:15:19a	36	06/28/11 01:15:49a	41
06/28/11 01:15:20a	36	06/28/11 01:15:50a	41
06/28/11 01:15:21a	36	06/28/11 01:15:51a	41
06/28/11 01:15:22a	36	06/28/11 01:15:52a	41
06/28/11 01:15:23a	36	06/28/11 01:15:53a	41
06/28/11 01:15:24a	32	06/28/11 01:15:54a	41
06/28/11 01:15:25a	32	06/28/11 01:15:55a	44
06/28/11 01:15:26a	32	06/28/11 01:15:56a	44
06/28/11 01:15:27a	29	06/28/11 01:15:57a	44
06/28/11 01:15:28a	29	06/28/11 01:15:58a	44
06/28/11 01:15:29a	29	06/28/11 01:15:59a	44

F. Movement Display

The system records information on the movement of each tractor through the GPS system.

```
QPADEV01VC OPM5X                                                                    2/23/04
SALDP                             Movement Display                                 15:50:58
                               From 11/01/03 To 2/23/04

For Driver - 918453
Trip   Load   Dest   Dead                Disp  Order    Di  P  MILES   Revenue Trip Drvg  Trip  Idle  PTO  Trip Bonus Ovspd
Origin City   City   Head   Trlr   Trac  Date  Number   sp  S  Ld  Dh  / MILE  MPG  MPG   Fuel  Fuel  Fuel Mles Amt   Time
OGDEUT OGDEUT SLC UT        T63277 28477 1229  H467161  01     32        1.110 4.16 6.10  71.5  22.7  22.2  298        .0
SLC UT SLC UT DELACA        T63277 28477 1230  H467161  02     732       1.110 5.61 6.82  93.1  16.5  16.1  523        .0
DELACA SFS CA WINCVA        542490 28477 1231  H512542  01     2566 156  1.273 7.02 7.41 418.7  22.0  21.3 2943        .1
WINCVA WINCVA MARTWV MARTWV 68512  28477 105   H516286  01     22        1.475 3.14 5.96  10.8   5.1   4.8   34        .0
MARTWV HAGEMD BRUNGA        T51932 28477 105   H527334  01     731  19   1.099 6.11 7.23 140.2  21.6  20.8  858        .0
BRUNGA AUGUGA CAMBOH        T51932 28477 107   H550430  01     550 185    .896 7.12 7.28 119.3   2.7   2.6  850        .0
CAMBOH MAS OH SUTHVA        T51932 28477 108   H550545  01     447  61   1.469 5.70 7.39 135.1  30.8  30.3  771        .0
SUTHVA CHEAVA PUEBCO        543783 28477 110   H566880  01     1755 94   1.371 5.86 6.17 368.8  18.3  18.1 2163        .0
PUEBCO PUEBCO HUTCKS        541145 28477 113   H614708  01     397       1.209 6.50 7.84  72.2  12.3  12.2  470        .0
HUTCKS MP  KS ANDRTX        72196  28477 113   H623375  01     608  33   1.711 6.17 7.27 122.7  18.5  17.8  758        .0
ANDRTX ODESTX NASHNN        72196  28477 115   H650533  01     2084 34   1.043 5.24 5.80 453.2  44.1  43.0 2376        .2
NASHNN LEOMMA GREENC GREENC 72196  28477 120   H645638  01     697  30    .992 6.56 7.09 155.7  11.7  11.5 1022        .1
GREENC RH  NC MOTONJ MOTONJ T62220 28477 121   H589010  01     485  36   1.582 6.53 7.87  99.0  16.8  16.6  647        .0
MOTONJ WHARNJ ATLAGA MEMPTN 72478  28477 123   H719827  01     823  66    .914 4.41 5.63 230.2  49.6  49.1 1017        .1

Earnings:  40,448.61  Deadhd  5 %  Driver Totals   30047   1563   1.280 6.08 6.75 6065.1 601.5 587.8 36926    1.6

F3=Exit F4=Ord Hst F6=Mult Eq     Order Nbr _____ Disp ___  Total Miles:  31610      16.8 %
```

G. SensorTrac Data

SensorTrac is a feature of the Qualcomm system that monitors speeds and idle time for vehicles as part of a fuel consumption program. The SensorTrac data can also be used to monitor drivers for hours of service and speeding issues.

```
SensorTRACS V2.1(0234)    OMVHDS v0031            02/24/04 09:53:11 MST
                 SensorTRACS PERFORMANCE DATA DIRECTORY

Type option and press ENTER.
  1=Select

                                                    Engine  OvSpd  Idle
Vehicle ID  Driver ID   Start Date    End Date  Dist  Hours    %     %
  28477     000918453  02/06/04 10:55 02/16/04 13:58    0     0    0.0  100.0
  28477     000918453  01/30/04 15:30 02/06/04 10:55  411    17    0.0   57.0
  28477     000918453  01/28/04 08:02 01/30/04 15:30  742    38    0.1   59.8
  28477     000918453  01/27/04 12:04 01/28/04 08:02  422    19    0.0   51.5
  28477     000918453  01/26/04 07:33 01/27/04 12:04  155    23    0.0   83.0
  28477     000918453  01/23/04 03:53 01/26/04 07:33 1017    75    0.5   72.6
  28477     000918453  01/21/04 18:28 01/23/04 03:53  647    31    0.1   58.8
  28477     000918453  01/20/04 06:21 01/21/04 18:28 1022    36    0.3   45.5
  28477     000918453  01/15/04 09:50 01/20/04 06:21 2376    92    0.3   52.9
  28477     000918453  01/13/04 19:33 01/15/04 09:50  758    34    0.2   57.7
  28477     000918453  01/12/04 21:08 01/13/04 19:33  470    22    0.0   57.0
  28477     000918453  01/10/04 10:14 01/12/04 21:08 2163    58    0.0   34.6
                                                                  More...

F1=Help   F3=Exit   F5=Refresh   F17=Top
```

H. VORAD

The VORAD (Vehicle Onboard Radar) is a warning system that can alert a truck driver when the vehicle is drifting out of its lane or if the truck is approaching a vehicle at an unsafe speed. The dashboard monitor issues an audible warning to the driver

Dashboard Monitor for VORAD

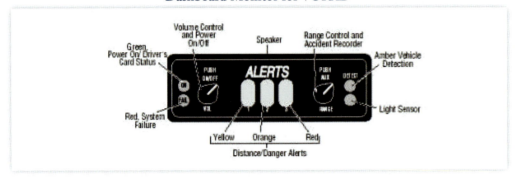

The VORAD's control module usually records data for 10 minutes preceding a collision including vehicle speed, turn signal status, brake status, turn rate and alert status. This data can be downloaded with the appropriate software.

VORAD Report

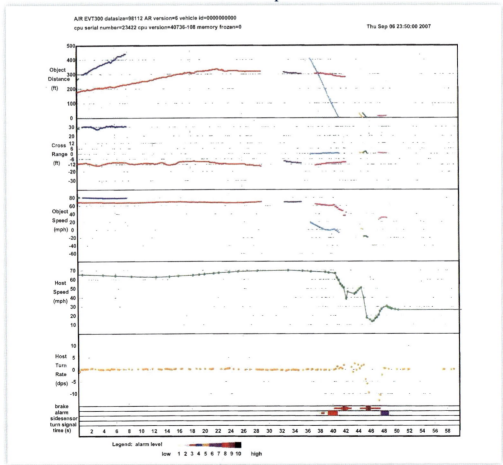

The VORAD report is a graph tracking various functions of the vehicle and system.

I. Dash Cam Videos

Many commercial vehicles now have dash cam video recorders installed in them. The recorder captures the roadway in front of the vehicle as well as what is going on inside the vehicle. The videos are uploaded to a website and stored there for a period of time. The recorder can include a function to automatically save and store video from a collision.

Dash Cam Video

This video is from a collision involving an ambulance.

J. Retention of Data

Messaging system data is destroyed as part of a normal document retention program. Each trucking company has a contract with the provider of the messaging system outlining what information and reports are available and how long they are kept. It is important to obtain a copy of this contract to determine what information is available for discovery. The electronic messages between the driver and dispatcher are kept the shortest amount of time which can be as short as 5 or

6 days. The SensorTrac reports are usually kept for 3 to 6 months. The other information including load information, driver master, tractor master, GPS tracking and movement display are usually kept for more than a year.

**Practice Pointer: Place the motor carrier on notice to print out Qualcomm data before it is destroyed and review the date for evidence of driver distraction, hours service violations and speeding.

X. Insurance Coverage

A. Minimum Insurance Requirements

Federal regulations require a motor carrier of non-hazardous property to have an insurance policy or surety bond in place in the amount of $750,000 to cover liability for injuries to the public.[587] A motor carrier transporting oil must have an insurance policy in place in the amount of $1 million dollars.[588] A carrier of certain hazardous materials must have insurance or a bond in the amount of $5 million dollars in liability coverage.[589] A carrier of passengers with a seating capacity of more than 15 must have $5 million dollars in insurance coverage and with a seating capacity of 15 or fewer must have $1,500,000 in insurance coverage.[590] Whenever an insurance policy and a governing statute requiring minimum insurance are in conflict, the statute controls and the policy is automatically amended by operation of law to conform the statutory minimum.[591] The minimum insurance requirements do not apply to reform excess or umbrella insurance policies.[592]

B. The MCS-90 Endorsement

The MCS-90 endorsement is required to be part of any insurance policy issued to a motor carrier in order to comply with federal minimum insurance requirements.[593] The endorsement states:

"In consideration of the premium stated in the policy to which this endorsement is attached, the insurer (the company) agrees to pay, within the limits of the liability described herein, any final judgment recovered against the insured for public liability resulting from the negligence in the operation, maintenance or use of motor vehicles subject to the financial responsibility requirements of Sections 29 and 30 of the Motor Carrier Act of 1980 regardless of whether or not each motor vehicle is specifically described in the policy and whether or not such negligence occurs on any route or in any territory authorized to be served by the insured or elsewhere. Such insurance as is afforded, for public liability, does not apply to injury to or death of the insured's employees while engaged in the course of their employment, or property transported by the insured, designated as cargo. It is understood and agreed that no condition, provision, stipulation, or limitation contained in the policy, this endorsement, or any other endorsement thereon, or violation thereof, shall relieve the company from liability or from the payment of any final judgment, within the limits of liability herein described, irrespective of the financial condition, insolvency or bankruptcy of the insured. However, all terms, conditions, and limitations in the policy to which the endorsement is attached shall remain in full force and effect as binding between the insured and the company. The insured agrees to reimburse the company for any payment made by the company on account of any accident, claim or suit involving a breach of the terms of the policy, and for any payment that the company would not have been obligated to make under the provisions of the policy except for the agreement contained in this endorsement…The limits of the company's liability for the amount prescribed in this endorsement apply separately to each accident and any payment under this policy because of any one accident shall not operate to reduce the liability of the company for the payment of final judgments resulting from any other accident."[594]

---

[587] 49 C.F.R. § 387.9.
[588] 49 C.F.R. § 387.9.
[589] 49 C.F.R. § 387.9.
[590] 49 C.F.R. § 387.33.
[591] Sonoco Products Co., Ins. v. Fire & Casualty Ins. Co. of Connecticut, 767 A.2d 1018 (N.J. 2001).
[592] Id.
[593] 49 C.F.R. § 387.15.
[594] 49 C.F.R. § 387.15.

MCS-90 Endorsement Filed with FMCSA Registration

Endorsement for Motor Carrier Policies of Insurance for Public Liability under Sections 29 and 30 of the Motor Carrier Act of 1980

FORM MCS-90

Issued to _____ of _____
 (Motor Carrier name) (Motor Carrier state or province)

Dated at _____ on this ___ day of _____, ___

Amending Policy Number: _____ Effective Date: _____

Name of Insurance Company: _____

Countersigned by: _____
 (authorized company representative)

The policy to which this endorsement is attached provides primary or excess insurance, as indicated for the limits shown (check only one):

○ This insurance is primary and the company shall not be liable for amounts in excess of $ _____ for each accident.

○ This insurance is excess and the company shall not be liable for amounts in excess of $ _____ for each accident in excess of the underlying limit of $ _____ for each accident.

This MCS-90 filing is required by the FMCSA.

The MCS-90 endorsement requires the insurer to act as a surety for any injury to the public caused by the carrier during interstate transportation and to be responsible for a judgment against the carrier even though no coverage may exist under the policy issued by the insurer.[595] The primary purpose of the MCS-90 endorsement is to assure that injured members of the public are able to satisfy a judgment from negligent interstate carriers.[596] The MCS-90 endorsement does not create coverage where it did not formerly exist but only imposes a reimbursable obligation as to final judgments rendered against the named insured.[597] The MCS-90 endorsement is usually not applicable if there is adequate insurance coverage to cover the loss.[598] Pursuant to the terms of the endorsement, an insurer is required to satisfy a judgment against the motor carrier even if the vehicle involved in the accident is not listed as a scheduled auto.[599] The responsibility is on the motor carrier, and not the insurer, to obtain the endorsement, and the insurance contract cannot be reformed to include the MCS-90 if the motor carrier did not request it.[600] If the insurer does not know that the trucking company is operating in interstate commerce, then the MCS-90 endorsement is not read into the policy.[601]

When the policy is issued to the trucking company operating the vehicle, the MCS-90 endorsement traditionally only applies to judgments against the named insured and not to permissive users[602] or drivers even if the drivers are employees of the carrier.[603] However, the MCS-90 endorsement has been expanded to collect a judgment against a corporation when the policy is issued to the corporation's sole shareholder and the plaintiff pierces the corporate veil.[604]

---

[595] Canal Insurance Co. v. Carolina Casualty Insurance Co., 59 F.3d 281 (1st Cir. 1995); T.H.E. Insurance Co. v. Larsen Intermodal Services, Inc., 242 F.3d 667 (5th Cir. 2001).

[596] Adams v. Royal Indemnity Co., 99 F.3d 964 (10th Cir. 1996).

[597] Harco National Insurance Co. v. Bobac Trucking, Inc., 107 F.3d 733 (9th Cir. 1997); Auto-Owners Insurance Co. v. Munroe, 614 F.3d 322 (7th Cir. 2010).

[598] Great West Casualty Co. v. General Casualty Co. of Wisconsin, 734 F.Supp.2d 718 (D.Minn. 2010).

[599] John Deere Insurance Co. v. Nueva, 229 F.3d 853 (9th Cir. 2000); Adams v. Royal Indemnity Co., 99 F.3d 964 (10th Cir. 1996).

[600] Illinois Central Railroad Co. v. DuPont, 326 F.3d 665 (5th Cir. 2003).

[601] Waters v. Miller, 560 F.Supp.2d 1318 (M.D.Ga. 2008).

[602] Del Real v. U.S. Fire Insurance Crum & Forster, 64 F.Supp.2d 958 (E.D. Cal. 1998); Armstrong v. United States Fire Insurance Co., 606 F.Supp.2d 794 (E.D.Tenn. 2009).

[603] Perry v. Harco National Insurance Co., 129 F.3d 1072 (9th Cir. 1997).

[604] Miller v. Harco Insurance Co., 522 S.E.2d 848 (Ga. 2001).

In 2005, the FMCSA issued an advisory opinion attempting to limit the scope of the MCS-90 endorsement.[605] The advisory opinion states as follows:

Q: Does the term "insured," as used on Form MCS-90, Endorsement for Motor Carrier Policies of Insurance for Public Liability, or "Principal", as used on Form MCS-82, Motor Carrier Liability Surety Bond, mean the motor carrier named in the endorsement or surety bond?

A: Yes. Under 49 C.F.R. 387.5, "insured and principal" is defined as "the motor carrier named in the policy of insurance, surety bond, endorsement, or notice of cancellation, and also the fiduciary of such motor carrier." Form MCS-90 and Form MCS-82 are not intended, and do not purport, to require a motor carrier's insurer or surety to satisfy a judgment against any party other than the carrier named in the endorsement or surety bond or its fiduciary.

Since this advisory opinion, the Courts have consistently held that the MCS-90 endorsement only applies to judgments against the named insured motor carrier and no one else.[606]

The MCS-90 endorsement only applies to interstate carriers and policies issued to comply with federal regulations.[607] The vehicle must have actually crossed state borders or was intended to cross state borders as part of the route,[608] and the vehicle must have been used to transport property or passengers by a for-hire carrier at the time of the collision for the MCS-90 to be applicable.[609] The MCS-90 endorsement does not apply to shipments in intrastate commerce even if transported by a carrier with interstate authority,[610] but does apply to the transportation of an exempt commodity in interstate commerce.[611] The endorsement applies once per accident and not per person[612] and only applies once per motor carrier even if there are multiple policies issued to the carrier.[613] However, the MCS-90 endorsement may be utilized separately for each different motor carrier with liability for the accident.[614] The endorsement does not control disputes among multiple insurers over which insurer should bear the ultimate financial burden for the loss, and the terms of the policies will control the issue of which policy provides primary coverage.[615] An insurer cannot in good faith refuse to pay a judgment against a trucking company when the MCS-90 endorsement is part of the policy.[616]

A State Public Service Commission may adopt regulations requiring an endorsement similar to the MCS-90 for insurance policies for intrastate carriers, and this endorsement will require an insurer to be responsible for a judgment against a carrier regardless of whether the vehicle involved in the accident is a scheduled auto.[617] State regulations also make an insurer liable for a loss to the extent of the minimum limits of required insurance coverage regardless of the actual policy limit.[618]

Practice Pointer: If there are any coverage defenses, try to utilize the MCS-90 endorsement to pursue a recovery.

---

[605] 70 FR 58065-01.
[606] Illinois National Insurance Co. v. Temian, 779 F.Supp.2d 921 (N.D.Ind. 2011); Forkwar v. Progressive Northern Insurance Co., 910 F.Supp.2d 815 (D. Md. 2012); McComb v. National Casualty Co., 994 F.Supp.2d 918 (2013).
[607] Canal Insurance Co. v. Barker, 358 Fed. Appx. 470 (4th Cir. 2009).
[608] Progressive Gulf Insurance Co. v. Jones, 958 F.Supp.2d 706 (S.D.Miss. 2013).
[609] Canal Insurance Co. v. YMV Transport, 867 F.Supp.2d 1099 (W.D.Wash. 2011); Martinez v. Empire Fire and Marine Insurance Co., 94 A.3d 711 (Conn. 2014).
[610] Progressive Casualty Insurance Co. v. Hoover, 768 A.2d 1157 (Penn. 2001); QBE Insurance Co. v. P & F Container Services, Inc., 828 A.2d 935 (N.J. 2003).
[611] Royal Indemnity Co. v. Jacobsen, 863 F.Supp. 1537 (D.Utah 1994); Century Indemnity Co. v. Carlson, 133 F.3d 591 (8th Cir. 1998).
[612] Carolina Casualty Insurance Co. v. Karpov, 559 F.3d 621 (7th Cir. 2009).
[613] Carolina Casualty Insurance Co. v. Yeates, 584 F.3d 868 (10th Cir. 2009).
[614] Herrod v. Wilshire Insurance Co., 737 F.Supp.2d 1312 (D.Utah 2010).
[615] Canal Insurance Co. v. First General Insurance Co., 889 F.2d 604 (5th Cir. 1989); Occidental Fire & Casualty Co. of N.C. v. International Insurance Co., 804 F.2d 983 (7th Cir. 1986); John Deere Insurance Co. v. Truckin' USA, 122 F.3d 270 (5th Cir. 1997); Carolina Casualty Insurance Co. v. Canal Insurance Co., 940 F.Supp.2d 753 (S.D.Ohio 2013); Tri-National, Inc. v. Yelder, 781 F.3d. 408 (8th Cir. 2015).
[616] Canal Insurance Co. v. Distribution Services, Inc., 176 F.Supp.2d 559 (E.D. Va. 2001).
[617] Ross v. Stephens, 496 S.E.2d 705 (Ga. 1998).
[618] Id.

C. Cancellation of a Policy

The MCS-90 endorsement must specify that: "Cancellation of this endorsement may be effected by the company or the insured by giving (1) 35 days notice in writing to the other party (said 35 days notice to commence from the date the notice is mailed, proof of mailing shall be sufficient proof of notice), and (2) if the insured is subject to the FMCSA's jurisdiction by providing 30 days notice to the FMCSA (said 30 days notice to commence from the date the notice is received by the FMCSA at its office in Washington, D.C.)."[619] A failure to follow this procedure will result in the policy remaining in effect despite the insurer's intent to cancel the policy.[620]

Federal regulations require that certificates of insurance cannot be canceled or withdrawn until 30 days after written notice has been given to the Board by the insurance company, surety or sureties, motor carrier, broker or other party which period of 30 days shall commence to run from the date such notice on the prescribed form is actually received by the Board.[621] Certificates of insurance or surety bonds may be replaced by other certificates of insurance, surety bonds or other security and the liability of the retiring insurer or surety under such certificates of insurance or surety bonds is terminated as of the effective date of the replacement certificate of insurance provided the policy is acceptable to the Commission under the rules and regulations of this part.[622]

An insurer must also comply with state law regarding notice provisions before canceling a policy on file with a State Public Service Commission and a failure to give the notice required by State law can create continuous coverage despite the intent of the insurer to cancel the policy and the availability of other coverage.[623] State law may recognize a distinction between canceling an insurance policy and the expiration of the policy.[624] If the insured is engaged solely in intrastate commerce or the insured tells the insurer that it is not engaged in interstate commerce after such information is requested by the insurer, the insurer does not have to comply with federal regulations and only needs to meet the state law requirements.[625] However, a failure to cancel a policy in accordance with federal or state law provisions does not necessarily mean that the predecessor insurer's policy provides primary coverage in a dispute between insurers.[626]

Practice Pointer: If the amount of coverage is an issue, review filings with state agencies to make sure all predecessor policies were properly cancelled. If a former insurer failed to properly notify the state agency of the cancellation, the policy may still be in effect.

D. Trailer Policies

The owner of a trailer may have a policy of liability insurance providing coverage to a driver as a permissive user.[627] Even if the tractor and trailer are insured under the same policy, there may be separate limits of coverage for both the tractor and trailer (i.e. $1 million of coverage on each for a total of $2 million).[628] When the trailer owner is different than the tractor owner, the MCS-90 endorsement on a liability policy covering the trailer may be used to create an additional recovery up to the federal statutory minimum including an expansion of the definition of a permissive user found in the policy to include both the driver and the owner of the tractor.[629]

---

[619] 49 C.F.R. § 387.15.
[620] Luizzi v. Pro Transport, Inc., 548 F.Supp.2d 1 (E.D.N.Y. 2008).
[621] 49 C.F.R. § 387.313(d).
[622] 49 C.F.R. § 387.313(e).
[623] DeHart v. Liberty Mutual Insurance Co., 169 F.3d 727 (11th Cir. 1999).
[624] Waters v. Miller, 564 F.3d 1355 (11th Cir. 2009); But See Brown v. QBE Insurance Corp., 677 S.E.2d 363 (Ga. 2009).
[625] Howard v. Quality Xpress, Inc., 989 P.2d 896 (N.M. 1999).
[626] Canal Insurance Co. v. Insurance Co. of North America, 424 So.2d 749 (Fla. 1982).
[627] Wilshire Insurance Co. v. Sentry Select Insurance Co., 124 Cal. App.4th (2004); LaFleur v. AFTCO Enterprises, Inc., 927 So.2d 1200 (La. 2006).
[628] Auto-Owners Insurance Co. v. Anderson, 756 So.2d 29 (Fla. 2000); Lucero v. Northland Insurance Co., 326 P.3d 42 (NM 2014). But See Canal Insurance Co. v. Blankenship, 129 F.Supp.2d 950 (S.D.W.Va. 2001).
[629] Lynch v. Yob, 768 N.E.2d 1158 (Ohio 2002).

Practice Pointer: If there is an issue about the amount of coverage, review the trailer policy to determine if it provides extra coverage.

E. Lessor's Insurance

The lessor/owner of a tractor-trailer may purchase liability insurance to cover its vehicles even though the vehicles are leased to and operated by another company. The policy issued to the lessor/owner may provide coverage to a permissive driver as an additional insured under the policy even though the lessor/owner has no role in the transportation process and is not vicariously liable for the driver's conduct.[630] Depending on the situation, the lease agreement may limit the amount of coverage provided to the driver.[631]

F. Non-Trucking/Bobtail Policies

An owner of a tractor may purchase non-trucking/bobtail coverage. This coverage is intended to provide insurance when the tractor is not being operated in the business of or under dispatch from a trucking company, and the policy usually contains an exclusion to this effect. Most courts have upheld this exclusion as valid.[632] The reason that the exclusion does not violate public policy is because the federal scheme does not allow the driver to drive in an out of coverage. The trucking liability policy covers the driver when he is driving on the business of a trucking company and the non-trucking/bobtail coverage provides coverage in all other circumstances. There is no gap in coverage. At least one jurisdiction has found that the exclusion violates public policy but limits the amount of coverage to the state statutory minimum.[633] Most courts take a very expansive view of the phrase "in the business of" and hold that a truck is in the business of the trucking company until (1) returns to the place where the haul originated; (2) returns to the terminal from which the haul was dispatched, or (3) returns to the terminal from which the driver customarily is assigned hauls.[634] As such, non-trucking/bobtail policies rarely provide coverage for a loss.

G. Commercial General Liability Policies

Commercial General Liability ("CGL") policies are generally obtained by businesses to insure against injuries occurring on a business premises. The CGL policy typically has an exclusion for any injuries related to automobiles, including the unloading and loading of vehicles. Because of the auto exclusion, CGL policies usually do not provide coverage for a tractor-trailer accident even if it occurs on a business premises.[635] Even if negligent hiring or retention is alleged, the auto exclusion will exclude coverage for the loss.[636]

H. Passenger Exclusions

An exclusion of coverage for passengers in a commercial vehicle is valid and enforceable, but a policy with such an exclusion will still be conformed to provide the minimum amounts of coverage for commercial vehicles required by federal and state law when a passenger is injured in an accident.[637]

---

[630] LaFleur v. AFTCO Enterprises, Inc., 927 So.2d 1200 (La. 2006); Stan Koch & Sons Trucking, Inc. v. Great West Casualty Co., 517 F.3d 1032 (8th Cir. 2008).
[631] Cotton v. Commodore Express, Inc., 459 F.3d 862 (8th Cir. 2006).
[632] Integral Insurance Co. v. Maersk Container Service Co., 520 N.W.2d 656 (Mich. 1994); Connecticut Indemnity Co. v. Podeszwa, 921 A.2d 458 (N.J. 2007).
[633] Connecticut Indemnity Co. v. Hines, 40 A.D.3d 903 (N.Y. 2007).
[634] St. Paul Fire & Marine Ins. v. Frankhart, 370 N.E.2d 1058 (Ill. 1977); Auto-Owners Insurance Co. v. Redland Insurance Co., 522 F.Supp.2d 891 (W.D.Mich. 2007).
[635] Strickland v. Auto-Owners Insurance Co., 615 S.E.2d 808 (Ga. 2005); Federal Insurance Co. v. New Coal Co., Inc., 415 F.Supp.2d 647 (W.D.Va. 2006).
[636] Howell v. Ferry Transportation, Inc., 929 So.2d 226 (La. 2006).
[637] Guinn Transport, Inc. v. Canal Insurance Co., 507 S.E.2d 144 (Ga. 1998).

I. Direct Action against Insurer

Some jurisdictions allow a cause of action to be maintained against the insurer of a trucking company as a named party defendant whenever an accident occurs.[638] The rationale for allowing a direct action against the insurer is that the insurer acts as the surety of the trucking company for the benefit of the public since the trucking company could not obtain authority to operate in interstate commerce without filing its proof of insurance.[639]

This form is filed with the federal or state government as proof of financial responsibility by the insurance company.

Practice Pointer: If your jurisdiction has a direct action statute, always name the insurer as a party defendant.

---

[638] See O.C.G.A. § 40-2-140.
[639] Jackson v. Sluder, 569 S.E.2d 893 (Ga. 2002).

XI. Types of Trucking Cases

Each trucking case, like each automobile collision, is different. But trucking cases can be categorized into certain types that have similar issues. There are six general types of trucking cases: (1) Left Turns; (2) Underrides; (3) Stopped Trucks; (4) Rear End Collisions; (5) Improper Maneuvers; and (6) Cargo Shifts.

A. Left Turns

When a truck turns left in front of a passenger vehicle, the truck driver must have ample time to complete the turn without the passenger vehicle having to slam on brakes to avoid a collision. Because of the size and length of the tractor trailer and the heavily trafficked areas where deliveries are made, the truck driver must be patient and cautious before making a left turn. Many times drivers are in a hurry and attempt a left turn when they know the only way the turn can be safely made is if the approaching driver slows down and stops to avoid a collision. This kind of maneuver often leads to catastrophic results.

In left turn cases, driver fatigue is usually not an issue. The driver may have been distracted or inattentive but the fact that he was actually making a maneuver at the time of the accident is indicative that he was not asleep. Similarly, there are rarely problems with maintenance or repair of the vehicle since braking is not an issue. Instead, the driver will be subject to heavy cross-examination on the appropriateness of his maneuver given the instructions contained in the CDL Manual. There also may be issues of negligent hiring and retention if the driver has a history of improper maneuvers or accidents.

B. Underrides

When a tractor-trailer makes a turn or a maneuver which causes the trailer to block the roadway, there is always the potential that the driver of a passenger vehicle will not see the trailer in time to stop and will ride under the trailer. These collisions are usually fatal as the driver is decapitated by the side of the trailer.

Underride Accident

In this case, our client was catastrophically injured when a trailer was left across a roadway in heavy fog.

The most important issue in an underride case is the visibility of the trailer. The inquiry should focus on the lighting and weather conditions at the time of the accident and the lights, reflectors and retroreflective taping on the side of the trailer. It is important to photograph and perform an inspection of the trailer as soon as possible. Many times the trailer will have retroreflective taping on the side but there will be dirt or other material obscuring the taping. Conspicuity issues include the ability of the trailer to blend into the surroundings so that the approaching driver does not recognize the trailer across the roadway and instead believes he is seeing the bridge or overpass that is normally in that area.

Conspicuity Issues

A driver may fail to recognize a trailer in the roadway in the dark because it looks like the bridges or overpasses in the area that are familiar to the driver.

C. Stopped Trucks

A tractor-trailer that is stopped in or on the side of the roadway is always a potential hazard. Motorists approaching from the rear often fail to see the vehicle until it is too late to avoid a collision. Federal regulations require drivers to place warning markers behind their stopped vehicle to alert motorists of the tractor-trailer's presence in order to alleviate the risk of running into the rear of the stopped trailer.

Warning Triangles

We have handled many cases where the truck driver's failure to place warning markers contributed to a motorist colliding with the rear of the trailer.

The issue in colliding with a stopped truck case is how long the vehicle had been stopped and whether the markers had been placed appropriately. Under the FMCSR, the driver should immediately activate his hazard lights and then place caution markers behind his vehicle once he is stopped. The driver will inevitably claim he had just stopped his vehicle prior to the collision and did not have time to place the warning markers. It is important to obtain cellphone records, 911 call reports and Qualcomm messages to determine how long the driver was stopped in the roadway.

D. Rear End Collisions

The most prevalent type of truck case is where the tractor-trailer rear ends a stopped or slowing passenger vehicle. In this situation, the lawyer is faced with a multitude of potential issues. The truck driver may have fallen asleep or been fatigued so his drivers logs must reviewed for potential hours of service violations. The tractor-trailer may have been overweight. The truck driver's weight tickets must be obtained to see if the weight of the vehicle played any role in the accident and his prior history of overweight citations must be looked at to see any pattern of abuse. The tractor-trailer's brakes may have failed or may have been out of adjustment so the vehicle needs to be inspected and repair and maintenance records must be reviewed. The truck driver may have been speeding and ECM data or a good accident reconstructionist can show whether speed was a contributing cause to the collision.

E. Improper Maneuvers

Many accidents occur when the truck driver makes an improper lane change, fails to obey a stop light or stop sign or fails to maintain his lane. These cases often involve driver fatigue issues, and the lawyer needs to explore any potential hours of service violations. The driver may have a history of traffic violations and erratic maneuvers which will lead to a claim for negligent hiring or retention. The lawyer will need to retain an accident reconstructionist to examine the scene and inspect the vehicles to make sure the evidence is preserved to prove how the accident occurred.

F. Cargo Shifts

When a vehicle is improperly loaded, the load may shift when a tractor-trailer is coming around a curve causing the tractor-trailer to jackknife or overturn. The truck driver will usually tell the investigating officer that something unusual with the load caused the vehicle to behave strangely leading to the accident. However, it should be remembered that the truck driver will often blame the load when in actuality the vehicle overturned because he drove too fast into the curve. In such a situation, the lawyer should consider a claim against both the motor carrier and the shipper. It is important to preserve through photographs and otherwise any evidence about how the load was secured and to determine if the truck driver was exceeding the speed limit. If the truck driver was exceeding the speed limit, there is rarely a claim for improper loading. However, if the truck driver was below the speed limit for the curve, and you can prove that the trailer was loaded improperly and shifted during the maneuver, then you potentially have a claim for improper loading. If you do not have evidence of the manner in which the load was placed onto the trailer and secured, it is impossible to prevail on this claim which demonstrates the importance of preserving this evidence.

XII. Handling a Trucking Case

A. Accident Investigation

The first step in properly handling a trucking case is to retain an accident reconstructionist to investigate the accident scene, photograph and document the physical evidence and discover as much information as possible from the investigating officers. Skid marks and other physical evidence begin to fade and disappear within days after the accident depending on the weather conditions. If you can retain a qualified reconstructionist and have him at the scene within 48 hours of an accident, you have a strong likelihood of being able to independently document skid mark lengths and measurements and other physical evidence. After this time period has expired, your reconstructionist will have to rely on the painted marks left at the scene by the investigating officers and the measurements obtained during their investigation as a basis for estimating speeds and movements of vehicles. You should make every attempt to have a reconstructionist examine the accident scene as soon as possible.

When a commercial vehicle is involved in a serious accident, the DOT, PSC or FHWA will usually conduct a post-accident inspection of the tractor and trailer. This inspection will document any problems with the unit, especially any problems with the braking system or tires. However, the purpose of the governmental post-accident inspection is to determine the extent of any mechanical problems with the vehicle and decide whether or not to place it out-of-service. The safety inspector is not trying to determine the cause of the accident. In order to further understand the cause of the accident, your reconstructionist, or a separate trucking expert depending on the reconstructionist's qualifications, will need to inspect the vehicles involved in the accident and document the results of his inspection.

B. Preservation of Evidence

You should send a spoliation letter to the trucking company and its insurer listing all documents and physical evidence to be preserved and maintained after the accident. A sample spoliation letter is contained in the Appendix, XVIII-1. The letter must state that the company keep all documents related to the unit and driver for the one-year period prior to the accident and outline the importance of these documents to your client's cause of action. It is crucial in cases alleging a manufacturing defect that the rear guard, tow bar, or other allegedly defective parts are kept and maintained.

You should also request that the company preserve the electronic control module ("ECM") on the tractor for later examination. The ECM controls the systems on the tractor unit, and electronically records data concerning the operation of the tractor including speeds, brake system operations and engine controls. This information can be downloaded by the manufacturer and could be vital in determining the mechanical condition and performance of the unit at the time of the accident. Manufacturers began routinely using electronically controlled systems on tractors starting in the mid-1990's, and most units currently on the road have an ECM.

In addition to sending a spoliation letter, you should contact the appropriate state agency to obtain copies of any filings and certificates concerning the trucking company. Also send a Freedom of Information Act (FOIA) request to the FMCSA to obtain as much information as possible on the motor carrier. A sample FOIA request is contained in the Appendix, XVIII-2. It is also important to go onto the Safer website and download the information concerning safety inspections on the trucking company since this information only goes back for a two-year period on the website.

C. The Complaint

Before filing your complaint against the trucking company, you should analyze the possibility of also bringing a products liability action against the manufacturer of the tractor, trailer or any component part within the unit. You should analyze the viability of a claim against the broker or shipper and the possibility of bringing an action against the insurance company for negligent hiring of the driver if a small trucking company is involved. If your jurisdiction has a direct action statute, you should name the insurer as a party defendant in addition to the trucking company. You should include in your complaint all applicable theories of liability including: (1) Negligent hiring, entrustment or retention, (2) Negligent inspection, maintenance or repairs, (3) Violations of the FMCSR, (4) Driver fatigue, and (5) Punitive damages.

D. Discovery

During the course of discovery, you should serve requests for the following documents: (1) Driver's qualification file; (2) Driver's logs for at least the eight day period preceding the accident; (3) Daily inspection reports for the three month period preceding the accident, (4) Annual inspection report covering the date of the accident, (5) Inspection, maintenance and repair records for the one year period preceding the accident and the six month period subsequent to the accident, (6) Printouts or data from on-board recording devices, (7) Downloadable data from the ECM, (8) Post-accident drug and alcohol tests, (9) Accident register for the time period preceding the accident, (10) Bills of lading, weight tickets, hotel receipts and similar documents for the eight day period preceding the accident, (11) Policy and procedure manuals, and (12) Training documents. You should take the deposition of the safety director, who is the person designated by the trucking company to be in charge of its safety program. The safety director should be questioned at length about the company's hiring criteria in general and as it applies to the driver involved in the accident, the company's safety records, its safety policies and procedures and its methods of monitoring its drivers.

E. Trucking Experts

You will inevitably need at least one trucking expert to assist you in prosecuting your case. The key is determining the issues presented by the facts of your case, and then retaining the most qualified expert on each issue. At bare minimum, you will need an accident reconstructionist to help you recreate the accident and the speeds and movements of the vehicles. You can also expect to retain a trucking expert for issues of conspicuity, mechanical failures, defective parts, driver fatigue, negligent hiring and retention, and compliance with federal regulations.

**Practice Pointer: Learn what are the important issues in your cases and determine if you need expert testimony to explain the issues to a jury.

XIII. Other Types of Accidents Related to Commercial Vehicles

A. Forklift Accidents

There are two different types of forklift accidents that can occur during the process of loading or unloading a tractor-trailer. The first type of accident involves the tractor-trailer rolling away from the loading dock while the forklift is attempting to enter or exit the trailer. In this scenario, the forklift falls in between the loading dock and the trailer causing the operator to become injured from the force of the impact of hitting the ground. The second type of accident involves the floor of the trailer collapsing or having the landing gear collapse on the trailer when there is no tractor under the trailer and the trailer tipping to one side. The forklift operator may be injured by the impact or the broken wood of the trailer or from having his arm crushed between the forklift and the trailer.

OSHA regulations require that chocks be placed under the tires of a tractor and the parking brake set when loading a trailer that is attached to a tractor by forklift. "The brakes of highway trucks shall be set and wheel chocks placed under the rear wheels to prevent the trucks from rolling while they are boarded with powered industrial trucks."[640] OSHA regulations generally apply to the employer and its employees at the loading dock which would place the duty on the forklift driver to make sure the wheels are chocked and the parking brake is set.[641] However, most loading docks have signs and general practices in place requiring the truck driver to set the brake and chock the tires. The presence of such a practice would place a common law duty on the truck driver to follow the instructions at the loading dock, and a jury would have to weigh the comparative negligence of the forklift operator in failing to follow OSHA regulations with the truck driver's failure to follow industry standards. Many loading docks have also gone to mechanical devices that lock into the trailer that make it impossible for the trailer to roll away from the loading dock to alleviate the need for chocks.

When chocks aren't placed behind the tractor tires, the trailer can roll away causing the forklift to fall out the back of the trailer.

---

[640] 29 C.F.R. § 1910.178(k)(1).
[641] Zorgdrager v. State Wide Sales, Inc., 489 N.W.2d 281 (1992).

The scenario may also exist where the truck driver attempts to pull away from the loading dock before the forklift operator is finished loading or unloading the trailer, and the forklift falls in between the dock and the trailer. Each loading dock has its own policies and procedures that dictate when the loading or unloading process is complete and provides a signal to the driver to show that he is authorized to drive away from the dock. These policies can include a green or red light in front of the driver, the placement of cones in front of the vehicle until the loading or unloading process is concluded or other similar measures. When the driver leaves the loading dock prematurely, the only issue in the case is whether the facility failed to follow the appropriate procedure in place for notifying the driver or whether the driver failed to follow the signals given by the facility.

In addition to the trailer rolling or moving away while attached to a tractor, the trailer can also have a structural or mechanical defect where the floor of the trailer collapses under the weight of the forklift or the landing gear collapses causing the trailer to tip forward or to the side if it is not attached to a tractor when it is being loaded or unloaded. The trucking company and driver are required to perform various inspections on the trailer to look for structural issues with the trailer, but it is often difficult to see a problem with the floor unless there are pieces of wood that are missing from the floor or holes in the wooden floor. If the landing gear is bent or rusted out, it should be caught on a visible inspection. The landing gear will often be difficult to raise and lower if there is a problem with the gears inside the leg. Most loading facilities have jockey trucks that move the trailers around and may damage the landing gear by dragging it on the ground. If the problems with the trailer could have been discovered based on a visual inspection, then there exists a claim against the truck driver who dropped the trailer and the owner or operator of the trailer for failing to perform appropriate inspections on the trailer.

The landing gear on the trailer can collapse if the trailer is not attached to a tractor while the trailer is being loaded.

    If the problem with the trailer could not have been discovered with an appropriate inspection, then the only avenue of recovery is a claim for a breach of warranty against the owner of the trailer. Most jurisdictions recognize that the owner of the trailer warrants that the trailer is fit for the purpose for which it is being used, i.e. has no structural defects that would affect the ability to load the trailer with a forklift.[642] This warranty may be disclaimed by contract between the trailer owner and the loading facility.[643] If the warranty has not been disclaimed, then the forklift operator can bring an action for breach of warranty for having a structural defect with the trailer.[644]

Practice Pointer: Forklift cases are not easy because of the OSHA regulations placing a duty on the forklift operator to chock the tires. Make sure you can show that the truck driver and trucking company were responsible for chocking the tires under the practices at the loading dock or were responsible for the issue that led to the accident.

B. Garbage Truck Accidents Involving Pedestrians

The main issue with garbage trucks is dealing with pedestrians who may be in the area where the garbage truck is being operated. The garbage truck is a slow-moving vehicle that makes frequent stops within areas that are highly populated. The garbage truck operator is often required to back up in parking lots and streets without much visibility or space. Garbage trucks are usually equipped with a camera system that allows the driver to see the areas behind the truck. If the cameras are not operating correctly, the driver may not be able to see pedestrians to the rear of his vehicle. Any mechanical issue with the backup camera can be the basis of a negligence claim, and the camera should be inspected after a pedestrian accident to make sure it was operating correctly.

This camera had a defect with the lens causing a blurred area in the middle of the picture that allowed a pedestrian to be struck by the garbage truck.

Some garbage trucks are equipped with mechanical arms. The operator sits on the right side of the vehicle and has no other employee with him and instead relies on a joystick to operate the mechanical arm which picks up the can and dumps the contents into the back of his vehicle. The operator has to be certain that all pedestrians are clear of the area in order to make sure no one is struck by the mechanical arm or garbage can during this process.

---

[642] O.C.G.A. § 44-12-63 (3).
[643] Mercedes-Benz Credit Corp. v. Shields, 199 Ga. App. 89, 403 S.E.2d 891 (1991).
[644] Perton v. Motel Props, 230 Ga. App. 540, 497 S.E.2d 29 (1998).

The mechanical arm can lift the trash can without the garbage truck driver exiting the vehicle. The driver has to be certain that no pedestrians are close enough to be struck by the arm or garbage can.

Most garbage trucks are equipped with warning alarms when the truck is backing up or the arms on the front of the truck are lifting a dumpster. There is usually no alarm when using a mechanical arm to pick up a residential trash can from the side of the truck. In a pedestrian accident, the garbage truck company will argue that the alarm should have warned the pedestrian to move away from the garbage truck. However, many times the pedestrian cannot hear the alarm over other background noise and cannot appreciate that the alarm is indicating that the garbage truck is coming towards them versus just being operated in the general area. People are used to hearing noises and beeps and alarms and are not expected to run from the scene without some other indicator that they are in danger. In addition, the alarm system should always be tested after the accident to see if it actually was working at the time of the incident.

**Practice Pointer: Always inspect the cameras and backup alarms on the garbage truck as soon as possible after a pedestrian accident.

C. Disabled Passengers on a Transit Bus

The American with Disabilities Act (ADA) requires transit companies to make reasonable accommodations for disabled passengers on buses to provide them with an acceptable means of transportation.[645] Many jurisdictions place a duty of extraordinary care on the transit company or require the transit company to exercise the highest degree of care to protect the passengers from injury.[646] Most transit companies have surveillance videos on their buses to provide oversight and monitoring of the bus operators. These surveillance videos usually provide first hand evidence of what happened in an incident.

The surveillance video in the bus captured the passenger's fall and the fact that the bus driver never left her seat.

There are numerous policies and procedures and industry standards that govern the appropriate ways to assist disabled passengers. The transit company should have training material that instructs its drivers on how to provide assistance to disabled passengers and how to comply with the ADA. The main issues that arise in providing assistance is helping people up and down the stairs, assisting wheelchair patrons or people who have severely impaired mobility onto the bus by using the automated lift platform and securing them into their seats, and helping passengers with mental or visual impairments. The bus operator should always be out of his seat helping the passenger or being near them whenever a passenger is getting onto or off of the bus.

**Practice Pointer: Make sure to put the bus company on notice of the need to preserve the surveillance videos on the bus as soon as possible.

---

[645] 49 C.F.R. § 37 et. seq.
[646] O.C.G.A. § 46-9-1.

XIV. Principles of Accident Reconstruction in Commercial Vehicle Cases

In most commercial accidents, it will be necessary to retain the services of an accident reconstructionist to inspect the scene and vehicles and download any electronic information contained in the vehicle's systems. It is important to understand some of the basic principles involved in accident reconstruction to make sure your expert's opinions make sense and comply with physics and accepted principles of reconstruction.

A. Skidmarks and Physical Evidence at the Scene

Because skidmarks disappear from the roadway within days of a collision, it is important to have the accident reconstructionist go to scene and preserve the physical evidence on the roadway within a week of the accident if possible.

These skidmarks helped demonstrate which vehicle crossed the centerline prior to impact.

The accident reconstructionist should take photos of all the marks and physical evidence left on the roadway and survey the scene in order to create a scale diagram of the area. If the accident occurred more than a month before the lawyer is retained in the case, there is no reason to rush to have the accident reconstructionist survey the scene unless the accident occurred in a construction zone where the layout of the area may change. After a month, there is no chance of the marks being present in the roadway unless it is a very rural and untraveled area.

B. Area of Impact

The area of impact is normally determined by the presence of a gouge mark. When two vehicles collide, one of the vehicles is normally pushed down causing a scuff mark or gouge mark as the metal frame digs into the asphalt.

Gouge Mark

This gouge mark was definitive on the location of the vehicles at impact.

If there is no gouge mark, then the next method of determining the area of impact is to look at the debris field. When two vehicles impact, there is normally a debris field of broken glass and metal in the area.

Debris Field

The impact occurred in the general area where the debris field is located.

While it is not as definitive, the debris field can be used to locate the general area of impact between the vehicles.

C. Lights on the Vehicle

In nighttime collisions involving a disabled or slow-moving vehicle, there is often an issue as to whether to not the lights were on the vehicle that was struck by the tractor-trailer. If the vehicle has LED lights rather than normal halogen headlights, then there is no way to know if the lights were on at the time of the collision. However, halogen lights and electric bulbs (which are the typical lights used on a vehicle) have a filament that can be used to determine if the lights were on at the time of the collision. When the lights are on, the filament is warm and has the ability to stretch in a collision instead of breaking. If the filament is stretched, then the lights were on at the time of the collision. If the lights are off and the filament is cold, the filament will often break during a collision. The blinking of hazard lights are sufficient to warm the filaments and so the same rule is applicable to whether or not hazard lights were activated and blinking at the time of the collision. Your accident reconstructionist should photograph all the bulbs and filaments on the vehicle if there is an issue as to whether or not the lights were on at the time of the collision.

D. Electronic Control Module

The Electronic Control Module (ECM) is the "black box" of the tractor and should always be downloaded. The ECM data is so important that we have an entire section of the book dedicated to understanding the ECM data. Make sure your reconstructionist downloads the ECM or obtains a copy of the download from the defense side to interpret the data.

E. Airbag Module on Client's Vehicle

While we always want to download the ECM from the tractor-trailer, it is also important to locate your client's vehicle and download the airbag module. If the vehicle is equipped with an airbag module, there is a possibility that the collision could have activated the airbag module and recorded data for the seconds leading up to the collision. The airbag module can record the speed of the vehicle and whether or not the brakes were activated for up to 5 seconds

Airbag Module

CDR CRASH DATA RETRIEVAL

Multiple Event Data

Associated Events Not Recorded	0
Event(s) was an Extended Concatenated Event	No
An Event(s) was in Between the Recorded Event(s)	No
An Event(s) Followed the Recorded Event(s)	No
The Event(s) Not Recorded was a Deployment Event(s)	No
The Event(s) Not Recorded was a Non-Deployment Event(s)	No

System Status At AE

Low Tire Pressure Warning Lamp (If Equipped)	OFF
Vehicle Power Mode Status	Run
Remote Start Status (If Equipped)	Inactive
Run/Crank Ignition Switch Logic Level	Active

Pre-crash data

Parameter	-1.0 sec	-0.5 sec
Reduced Engine Power Mode	OFF	OFF
Cruise Control Active (If Equipped)	No	No
Cruise Control Resume Switch Active (If Equipped)	No	No
Cruise Control Set Switch Active (If Equipped)	No	No
Engine Torque (foot pounds)	137.93	139.41

Pre-Crash Data

Parameter	-2.5 sec	-2.0 sec	-1.5 sec	-1.0 sec	-0.5 sec
Accelerator Pedal Position (percent)	20	20	20	20	20
Vehicle Speed (MPH)	30	30	31	31	31
Engine Speed (RPM)	1792	1792	1856	1856	1856
Percent Throttle	36	36	36	36	36
Brake Switch Circuit State	OFF	OFF	OFF	OFF	OFF

The download shows the speed of 30 to 31 mph for 2.5 seconds and lack of braking on the client's vehicle before impact.

Like with the ECM, the data from the airbag module has to be interpreted by the reconstructionist. The zero point on the airbag download does not necessarily mean the point of impact. The zero point is only where the airbag module first woke up and started recording data, and the reconstructionist needs to take into account the type of collision and the physical evidence at the scene to see where in the process that the airbag module would have woken up.

F. Speed and Distance Analysis

The speed of a vehicle can be calculated using the standard formula:

$$\text{speed} = \sqrt{30 \times \text{distance} \times \text{coefficient of friction}}.$$

The coefficient of friction represents the amount of friction on the roadway. The most accurate way to determine the coefficient of friction is to drag a sled on the roadway which records the amount of friction. However, it is generally accepted that highway asphalt has a coefficient of friction in the range of 0.70 to 0.75. Distance is the amount of distance that the vehicle travelled from the time of braking until it comes to a stop. Normally this is determined by the length of the skidmarks left by the vehicle. The speed analysis is only relevant if you cannot determine the vehicle's speed from the download of the airbag module or the ECM. The electronic data is much more reliable than skidmark measurements and a speed analysis based on skidmarks.

G. Perception/Reaction Time

A reconstructionist should be able to use a speed and distance analysis along with perception/reaction time to determine where vehicles were at certain times prior to a collision and if there was sufficient time to take evasive maneuvers to avoid a collision. In a regular daytime scenario presented to a driver, a standard perception/reaction time is 1.5 seconds. The 1.5 seconds includes 1 second to see and perceive the danger and .5 seconds to move the foot to the brake and press it or to make an evasive maneuver. With a tractor-trailer driver, the perception reaction time is 1.75 seconds because there is a .25 second delay from when the brakes are pressed until the brakes actually engage on a tractor-trailer because of the air system that controls the brakes. A reconstructionist can determine where a tractor-trailer was prior to a collision by determining its speed prior to braking and moving the tractor-trailer backwards 1.75 seconds for perception/reaction time (for example at 55 mph a vehicle travels 88 feet per second for a total of 154 feet during the 1.75 second perception/reaction time). The importance of determining the location of vehicles prior to impact is to see if the truck driver was distracted so that he did not perceive and react to the danger in a reasonable manner (for example if the car was visible in the roadway for 1,000 feet but the truck driver did not perceive the vehicle until he was 500 feet from the vehicle, then there is a question as to why he did not see it sooner and slow down).

H. Re-Enactments and Simulations

Many accidents involve a tractor-trailer that is across the roadway either while making a turn or disabled for some reason. The claimant's vehicle collides with the tractor-trailer because the claimant fails to see the tractor-trailer in time to avoid running into it. These types of accidents always involve issues of visibility, especially when the collision occurs at night. The primary defense is that the claimant should have been able to see and avoid colliding with the tractor-trailer if the claimant had been paying attention while driving. As a result, it is imperative to re-enact the collision so that the jury can visually understand that anyone in the claimant's position would not have been able to recognize the tractor-trailer in time to take evasive action.

We performed a re-enactment of a collision where a tractor-trailer in a rural area was backing into a driveway when the claimant ran into the rear of the trailer which was in her lane of travel. By looking at the photographs of the re-enactment, it is evident that the tractor's headlights gave the appearance to the claimant that the tractor-trailer was approaching the claimant in the opposite lane of travel, and that it was impossible to see the trailer in the roadway until the claimant was less than 80 feet away.

A. 400 Feet

B. 200 Feet

C. 120 Feet

D. 80 Feet

E. 40 Feet

At 55 mph, the claimant traveled 88 feet in one second. Because a driver's perception/reaction time is longer at night, the claimant had no chance to perceive and react to the trailer before she collided with it. The re-enactment was critical to explaining this issue to the jury.

**Practice Pointer: Always consider a re-enactment of a nighttime driving accident.

A re-enactment is a necessity for a nighttime underride accident.

XV. Cellphone Evidence

The use of cellphones is one of the biggest distractions for truck drivers. The best evidence of cellphone use is a download of the cellphone itself. Because it is impossible to crack a password-protected smartphone without the password, the driver must provide his password in order to access the contents of the cellphone. If the driver refuses to give his password or suddenly cannot "remember" his password, then there is no reason to do anything with the cellphone itself other than to point out to the jury that the driver is most likely failing to remember his password because the contents of the cellphone are harmful to his defense of the case.

As long as the password is provided, you can hire a company to copy the contents of the phone and determine if the phone was in use at the time of the collision, including if the person was in the process of typing a text, was browsing the internet, was watching a video or doing anything else with their phone. The download of the phone is preferable to cellphone records because records only show completed texts and phone calls and not other cellphone activity. It is important to place the driver and company on notice to preserve the driver's cellphone for a later download at the beginning of a case. Because drivers sometimes have more than one cellphone, make sure you request that all cellphones "owned, operated or used" on the date of the accident are preserved.

If the cellphone cannot be downloaded, then the next best thing is to obtain the driver's cellphone records. You can only obtain cellphone records after a lawsuit has been filed by serving the cellphone provider with a subpoena. The cellphone records should include information about any texts sent or received, any phone calls made or received and cell tower information concerning the location of the person when the text or call was initiated.

The records show the texts and calls made and received. Make sure you know the time zone of the records.

You should always request 24 hours before the incident and 24 hours after the incident because many providers keep cell records in UTC time (Greenwich time zone). You will have to determine how to convert the UTC time in the cell records to the time zone in which the accident occurred.

In order to determine if the driver was using his cellphone at the time of the collision, it is necessary to know the exact time of the accident. The best evidence of the time of the collision is the initial 911 call. The 911 call log will have a specific time in terms of minutes and seconds when the initial call was made to 911.

911 Call Log

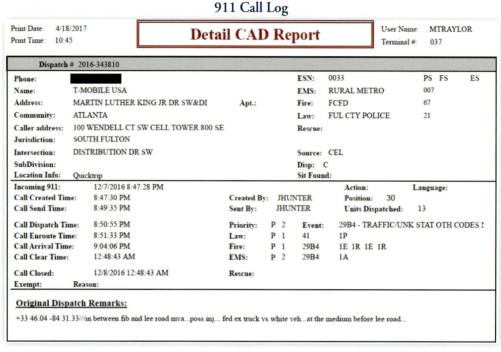

The initial 911 call will help determine the time of the collision.

You will then have to depose the witness who called 911 to determine the passage of time from when the impact occurred between the vehicles to when the 911 call was initiated by the witness. It is generally accepted that the accident will have occurred within a minute of the collision if the collision occurred on a busy interstate. However, in more rural areas, there can be a longer passage of time between the impact and the 911 call. If there was no 911 call, then you have to gather circumstantial evidence from the witnesses at the scene to determine when the accident occurred.

XVI. Deposing the Truck Driver & Safety Director

We have taken the transcripts for all of our truck driver and safety director depositions and placed them on a password-protected portal at **www.frg-law.com/portal**. Preparation is the key to taking a good deposition. You have to start the process by making sure you have obtained all the necessary documents from the trucking company. Then you have to sit down and analyze these documents and information to determine what issues you have in your case. Does your case involve an issue with driver's logs and hours of service? Does your driver have a bad driving history? Has the trucking company been monitoring its drivers appropriately? Your approach will be different depending on the answers to these kinds of questions and the specific issues in your case. A large part of the magic of being a trucking attorney is seeing and identifying these issues and putting together an approach for each one of them. However, there are some basic theories and questions that you will explore in every deposition. Those basic questions are discussed below.

A. The Truck Driver

Always depose the truck driver before the safety director. The questions that you will ask of the safety director will change depending on the testimony of the truck driver. If you take the depositions out of order, you will inevitably miss out on several questions for the safety director that only become applicable because of the truck driver's testimony. The focus of any truck driver deposition is the rules. The rules normally come from the CDL manual and from safety guides put out by the trucking company or the FMCSA. After you have obtained testimony from the truck driver as to how the accident occurred, you should question the driver as to the rules that are applicable to the specific scenario that confronted him. What are the rules in the CDL manual specific to this scenario? What does a safety conscious truck driver do in this scenario? If you fail to follow these rules, do you place everyone on the roadway at risk? Once you have locked the truck driver into agreeing with the rules applicable to his conduct, you only need to prove that the contrary occurred in your case to show that he was negligent.

In addition to the general rules based approach about his conduct, you will also need to cross-examine the truck driver about other areas of potential rules violations including:

1. Texting while driving;
2. Cellphone use while driving;
3. Use of on-board messaging systems while driving;
4. Internet and TV use while driving;
5. Documents that can prove the driver's whereabouts;
6. Medical issues;
7. Post-accident drug & alcohol testing;
8. Information on driver's application;
9. Prior accidents and moving violations;
10. Issues with prior employers;
11. Criminal history;
12. Accident review;
13. Discipline history;
14. Dispatch procedures;
15. Paperwork and computer entries.

These areas of inquiry can lead to the discovery of problems with the driver that were not readily apparent from reviewing the documents produced by the trucking company.

B. The Safety Director

You should send a notice for deposition for certain areas of inquiry from a corporate representative of the trucking company. These areas of inquiry should reflect the specific issues in your case but should always include (1) safe driving practices and procedures; (2) policies and procedures concerning safe driving practices; (3) compliance with state and federal regulations; (4) investigation into the accident; and (5) documents produced by the trucking company. Normally, the safety director is designated as the corporate representative on these issues.

The safety director deposition will consist of two general areas of questioning: (1) the rules applicable to the driver's conduct and (2) red flags that were missed by the company in regards to the driver. Similar to the truck driver deposition, you must establish the rules for the driver's conduct with the safety director. Not surprisingly, the safety director and the truck driver often have a different understanding of what rules are applicable. Since you have the specific testimony of the truck driver already on record, you can ask the safety director questions about whether the specific actions taken by the truck driver are dangerous or if they comply with the applicable rules. Many times the safety director will become your expert as he or she has to admit that what the truck driver did in a specific circumstance does not comply with the rules applicable to his conduct.

You will also want to explore any red flags about the truck driver that were missed by the trucking company. The defense wants the case to be about what happened in the seconds before the collision where the truck driver was faced with an emergency situation and simply made an error in judgment. From the plaintiff's side, you want to show that the errors were made by the trucking company days, weeks or months before the collision when they missed the red flags that could have prevented this accident from ever occurring. The real cause of the accident is the trucking company's failure to keep a watchful eye over its drivers and to look for red flags related to the driver's history and qualifications, his pattern of driving over hours of service, drug or alcohol use, driver distractions or other dangerous conduct.

Most companies perform a preventability analysis whenever there is an accident involving one of its drivers. It is important to ask the safety director about the preventability analysis. The analysis is designed to examine if the driver violated the company's policies and procedures or industry standards in order to determine if the accident could have been prevented. If the accident is deemed preventable, then the company will charge the driver with a violation that will result in some type of disciplinary action. If the accident is not preventable, then the driver did nothing wrong, and it is not held against him. The result of the preventability analysis is usually not admissible at trial because it is deemed a subsequent remedial measure.[647] However, testimony and documents related to a preventability analysis are always discoverable.[648]

---

[647] Bulger v. Chi. Transit Auth., 345 Ill. App. 3d 103, 111 (Ill. Court of Appeals 2003). Prescott v. CSX Transport, Inc., 2013 LEXIS 40438 (S.D. Ga. 2013).

[648] Laney v. Schneider Nat'l Carriers, Inc., 2010 U.S. Dist. LEXIS 120069 (N.D.O.K. 2010); Venator v. Interstate Res., Inc., 2015 LEXIS 146891 (S.D.G.A. 2015).

Preventability Analysis

File Type	Upload Date	Uploaded By	File Name	Original File Name
Accident Diagram	12/6/2017 11:55:20 AM		2017095017_Accident_Diagram_001.xlsx	accident diagram.xlsx
Picture	12/6/2017 11:59:22 AM		2017095017_Picture_001.jpg	20171130_091305_1512061423853_resized.jpg
Picture	12/6/2017 11:59:47 AM		2017095017_Picture_002.jpg	20171130_091247_1512061421812_resized.jpg
Picture	12/6/2017 12:00:32 PM		2017095017_Picture_003.jpg	20171130_091233_1512061419305_resized.jpg
Statement	12/6/2017 12:06:25 PM		2017095017_Statement_001.pdf	

Review

Recommendations: IRB participants were: ▮▮▮▮▮▮ We concluded from evidence this was preventable. The driver was at fault. The driver was suspended. He was put on an 2 week action plan.

Disciplinary Action: 687

Investigator Name:		Investigation Date: 11/30/2017
Supervisor Name:	Network ID:	Review Date: 12/6/2017 3:52:10 PM
Branch Manager Name:	Network ID:	Review Date: 12/6/2017 3:52:10 PM

The company performed a standard preventability analysis on this accident.

The reason that the courts allow an inquiry into a preventability analysis is that information related to the preventability analysis may be relevant to the case against the company. In addition, if the company takes a position that is contrary to the findings contained in the preventability analysis, the documents will become admissible for the purposes of impeachment. You should always request and obtain copies of all documents related to the preventability analysis of the accident by the company and question the safety director about the investigation and the findings related to the analysis.

XVII. Trucking Checklists

1. DRIVER APPLICATION CHECKLIST
(AT TIME OF HIRING - 49 CFR § 391.21(b))

1. ____NAME & ADDRESS OF MOTOR CARRIER: (49 CFR § 391.21(b)(1)

2. ____APPLICANT'S NAME, ADDRESS, DOB, & SSN: (49 CFR § 391.21(b)(2)

3. ____APPLICANT'S ADDRESSES FOR PRIOR 3 YEARS:
   (49 CFR § 391.21(b)(3)

4. ____APPLICATION SUBMISSION DATE: (49 CFR § 391.21(b)(4)

5. ____STATE, NUMBER, & EXPIRATION OF ALL CDLs:
   (49 CFR § 391.21(b)(5)

6. ____NATURE & EXTENT OF APPLICANT'S EXPERIENCE IN OPERATION OF MOTOR VEHICLES INCLUDING TYPE OF EQUIPMENT OPERATED:
   (49 CFR § 391.21(b)(6)

7. ____LIST OF ALL ACCIDENTS FOR PRIOR 3 YEARS INCLUDING DATE, NATURE, & IF ANY FATALITIES OR INJURIES: (49 CFR § 391.21(b)(7)

8. ____LIST OF ALL VIOLATIONS OF MOTOR VEHICLE LAWS/ORDINANCES RESULTING IN CONVICTION OR BOND FORFEITURE FOR PRIOR 3 YEARS: (49 CFR § 391.21(b)(8)

9. ____STATEMENT REGARDING ANY DENIAL/REVOCATION/SUSPENSION OF ANY LICENSE OR PERMIT: (49 CFR § 391.21(b)(9)

10. ____LIST OF EMPLOYERS FOR PRIOR 3 YEARS INCLUDING EMPLOYMENT DATES, REASON FOR LEAVING, WHETHER SUBJECT TO FMCSRs, & WHETHER SUBJECT TO ALCOHOL & CONTROLLED SUBSTANCE TESTING: (49 CFR § 391.21(b)(10)

11. ____FOR DRIVERS APPLYING TO OPERATE CMVs AS DEFINED BY PART 383, LIST OF EMPLOYERS FOR 7 YEAR PERIOD PRECEDING 3 YEARS LISTED ABOVE WITH EMPLOYMENT DATES & REASON FOR LEAVING: (49 CFR § 391.21(b)(11)

12. ____CERTIFICATION & SIGNATURE LINE: 49 CFR § 391.21(b)(12)

2. DRIVER QUALIFICATION FILE CHECKLIST
(49 CFR § 391.51)

1. ____APPLICATION (49 CFR § 391.21)

2. ____A COPY OF A 3 YEAR MVR AT TIME OF HIRE (49 CFR § 391.23)

3. ____PRIOR EMPLOYER SAFETY INQUIRY (49 CFR § 391.23)

4. ____A CERTIFICATE OF A ROAD TEST (49 CFR § 391.31) OR EQUIVALENT (49 CFR § 391.33)

5. ____TRAINING CERTIFICATE FOR ENTRY LEVEL DRIVERS ONLY (49 CFR § 380.509) (Note: This can also be maintained in the personnel file)

6. ____AN ANNUAL COPY OF MVR FOR PAST YEAR (49 CFR § 391.25)

7. ____A NOTE OF ANNUAL REVIEW BY MOTOR CARRIER (49 CFR § 391.25)

8. ____ANNUAL LIST OF TRAFFIC VIOLATIONS FROM THE DRIVER (49 CFR § 391.27)

3. ELECTRONIC DATA CHECKLIST

1. ____SAFER WEBSITE DATA ON TRUCKING COMPANY

2. ____ECM DOWNLOAD FROM TRACTOR

3. ____DASH CAM/SURVEILLANCE VIDEO

4. ____GPS DATA FROM TELEMATICS SYSTEMS

5. ____ELECTRONIC DRIVERS LOGS

6. ____DATA FROM COLLISION AVOIDANCE SYSTEMS

7. ____MESSAGING DATA FROM ONBOARD COMPUTER SYSTEM

8. ____CELLPHONE DOWNLOAD

9. ____INTERNAL E-MAILS

10. ____SOCIAL MEDIA POSTINGS BY TRUCK DRIVER

11. ____MEDIA ONLINE PHOTOGRAPHS & VIDEO

4. RECORD RETENTION CHECKLIST

Document	Retention Period	Regulation
DQ File	Employment +3 years	49 CFR § 391.51(c)
Medical Certificate	3 years	49 CFR § 391.51(d)
Annual Review Docs	3 years	49 CFR § 391.51(d)
Driver History File	Employment+3 years	49 CFR § 391.53(c)
Driver Logs	6 months from receipt	49 CFR § 395.8(k)(1)
Log Supporting Docs	6 months from receipt	49 CFR § 395.8(k)(1)
Alcohol Tests ≤ 0.02	5 years	49 CFR § 382.401(b)(1)
Positive Drug Tests	5 years	49 CFR § 382.401(b)(1)
Test Refusal Docs	5 years	49 CFR § 382.401(b)(1)
Accident Register	3 years from MVC	49 CFR § 390.15
DVIRs	3 months	49 CFR § 396.11(a)(4)
Roadside Inspection	1 year	49 CFR § 396.9(d)(3)(ii)
Annual Inspection	14 months	49 CFR § 396.21(b)

5. TRUCKING CLAIMS CHECKLIST

A. Investigation of Accident
    1. Retain Reconstruction Expert to Investigate Accident and Photograph Scene
    2. Retain Trucking Expert to Inspect Vehicle
    3. Obtain Post-Accident PSC, DOT or FHWA Inspection Reports

B. Preservation of Evidence
    1. Obtain Motor Carrier Certificates and Filings from State Agencies
    2. Send Spoliation Letter to Trucking Company and its Insurer
    3. Download ECM Data
    4. Download SMS Results on Trucking Company from Safer website

C. Complaint
    1. File Direct Action Against Insurer if allowed under State Law
    2. Determine Product Liability Claims against Manufacturer
    3. Examine Potential Claims against Broker or Shipper
    4. Find out if Insurer Screened Drivers
    5. Determine Theories of Liability against Trucking Company
        a. Negligent Hiring, Entrustment or Retention
        b. Negligent Inspection, Maintenance or Repair
        c. Violations of FMCSR
        d. Driver Fatigue
        e. Punitive Damages

D. Discovery
    1. Request all Documents Required by Federal Regulations
        a. Driver's Qualification File
        b. Driver's Logs
        c. Daily Inspection Reports
        d. Annual Inspections
        e. Maintenance and Repair Records
        f. Qualcomm and On-board Recording Devices
        g. Downloadable Data from ECM
        h. Post-Accident Drug and Alcohol Testing
        i. Accident Register
        j. Bills of Lading, Weight Tickets, Hotel Receipts

      k. Policy and Procedure Manuals

      l. Training Documents

   2. Take the Driver and Safety Director's Depositions

E. Trucking Experts: What Issues are in My Case?

   1. Industry Standards and Common Practices

   2. Operation of Commercial Vehicles

   3. Driver Fatigue/ Driver's Logs

   4. Compliance with Federal Regulations

   5. Negligent Hiring and Retention

   6. Inadequate Maintenance or Repairs

   7. Defective Parts or Mechanical Failures

XVIII. Appendix of Forms

Our forms can now be accessed at our password protected portal found at **www.frg-law.com/portal**. We have included below a sample spoliation letter and FOIA Request to FMCSA. All other forms can be accessed online.

XVIII-1. Sample Spoliation Letter

[*Date*]

CERTIFIED MAIL/RETURN RECEIPT REQUESTED

[*Trucking Company*]
[*Address*]

[*Truck Driver*]
[*Address*]

[*Insurance Company*]
[*Address*]

RE: **SPOLIATION LETTER / LETTER OF REPRESENTATION**

Our Client: [*Client Name*]
Date of Incident: [*Date of Incident*]

Dear Sir/Madame:

My law firm represents [*Client Name*] in regards to personal injuries resulting from a collision with [*Truck Driver*] at approximately [*Time*] on [*Date*] at [*Location*]. The purpose of this letter is to request the preservation of certain evidence related to this accident. If you fail to preserve and maintain this evidence, we will seek any sanctions available under the law. We specifically request that the following evidence be maintained and preserved and not be destroyed, modified, altered, repaired, or changed in any manner:

1. Post accident drug and alcohol testing results;

2. Bills of lading for any shipments transported by your driver for the day of the accident and the eight day period preceding the accident;

3. Any permits or licenses covering the vehicle or load on the day of the accident;

4. Your driver's daily logs or time cards for the day of the accident and the 30 day period preceding the accident;

5. Your driver's daily inspection reports for the day of the accident and the one month period preceding the accident;

Sample Spoliation Letter (continued)

6. Daily inspection reports for the tractor and trailer involved in this accident for the day of the accident and the one month period preceding the accident;

7. Maintenance, inspection, and repair records or work orders on the tractor and trailer for the day of the accident and for the 6 month period preceding the accident;

8. Annual inspection report for the tractor and trailer covering the date of the accident;

9. Your driver's complete driver's qualification file, including but not limited to:

    a. application for employment
    b. CDL license
    c. driver's certification of prior traffic violations
    d. driver's certification of prior accidents
    e. driver's employment history
    f. inquiry into driver's employment history
    g. pre-employment MVR
    h. annual MVR
    i. annual review of driver history
    j. certification of road test
    k. medical examiner's certificate
    l. drug testing records
    m. HAZMAT or other training documents;

10. Photographs of the vehicle involved in this accident or the accident scene;

11. Dash cam or any surveillance camera for the day of the accident and the 5 day period prior to the accident;

12. Any lease contracts or agreements covering your driver or the truck involved in this accident;

13. Any agreements regarding maintenance or operation of the truck involved in this accident;

14. The ECM (electronic control module) and any data or printout from on-board recording devices, including but not limited to the ECM, any Qualcomm or on-board computer, tachograph, trip monitor, trip recorder, trip master, or other recording device for the day of the accident and the six month period preceding the accident;

15. Any post-accident maintenance, inspection, or repair records or invoices in regard to the truck;

— continued

Sample Spoliation Letter (continued)

16. Any weight tickets, fuel receipts, or other records of expenses regarding your driver involved in this collision for the day of the accident and the 8 day period preceding the accident;

17. Any trip reports or dispatch records regarding your driver or the truck involved in this collision for the day of the accident and the 8 day period preceding this accident;

18. Any e-mails, electronic messages, letters, memos, or other documents concerning this accident;

19. Any driver's manuals, guidelines, rules or regulations given to your drivers;

20. Any reports, memos, notes, logs or other documents evidencing complaints about your driver;

21. Any DOT or PSC reports, memos, notes or correspondence concerning your driver or the truck involved in this accident;

22. Any downloadable computer data from the truck's computer system or the trucking company's satellite system, Qualcomm or other similar system for the day of the accident and the 30 day period preceding this accident and 5 day period subsequent to this accident;

23. Any messages or other data sent via on-board computer system, satellite tracking system, telephone, Qualcomm or other similar system or other device to or from the driver or tractor-trailer involved in this accident for the day of the accident and the 30 day period preceding this accident and 5 day period subsequent to this accident;

We also request that you make no changes, repairs or alterations to the tractor or trailer until our accident reconstructionist has had the opportunity to inspect and photograph it and that you do not make any changes to the ECM until a download has been completed under the supervision of our reconstructionist. Further, we request that any cellphone owned, used or operated by the truck driver on the day of the accident be maintained and preserved until the data on the cellphone is downloaded and copied. We will pay for a temporary phone for the truck driver if necessary.

We request that you contact us immediately to schedule the inspection of the tractor and trailer and the download of the truck driver's cellphone(s). Please govern yourself accordingly. If you have any questions, please do not hesitate to call.

Very truly yours,
[*Attorney Name*]

XVIII-2. Sample FOIA Request to FMCSA

[*Date*]

Federal Motor Carrier Safety Administration
Attn: FOIA, Team MC-MMI
400 7th Street, S.W.
Washington, DC 20590

RE: [Client Name v. Defendant Name/Company]

Company – *[Name of Trucking Company]*
DOT No. – [Trucking Company DOT Number]

Dear Sir/Madam:

Pursuant to 5 U.S.C. § 552 and 29 C.F.R. § 1610.7, we are submitting the following Freedom of Information Act request. In making this request, we hereby certify that we assume financial liability for the direct cost of the search for the requested records and their duplication as set forth in 20 C.F.R. § 1610.15. In the event that the Commission declines to provide certain of the requested documents, you should notify us of this decision and describe each document withheld. Otherwise, the following information should be made available within ten (10) working days after receipt of this request:

A copy of any inspection reports, logs, citations, insurance filings, disciplinary actions, licenses, authorities, correspondence, safety records, accident register or any other documents concerning, referencing, or relating to [*Trucking Company*].

We appreciate your cooperation in this matter and look forward to hearing from you in the very near future.

Very truly yours,

[*Attorney Name*]

XIX. Index

Accident Investigation 119
Accident Reconstruction 127-134
    Airbag Module 130
    Area of Impact 128
    Lights Activated on Vehicle 129
    Perception/Reaction Time 131
    Reenactments 131-134
    Skidmarks 127
    Speed Calculations 131
Accident Register 77
Agent for Service of Process 15
Airbag Module 130
Alcohol & Controlled Substances 55-65
    Admissibility 63
    Alcohol, Use of 55
    Chain of Custody 59-62
    Controlled Substances, Use of 56
    Medical Review Officer (MRO) 60-62
    Policies & Procedures 63-64
    Post-Accident Testing 58
    Pre-employment Screening 56-57
    Random Testing 58
    Reasonable Suspicion Testing 57
    Record Retention 64-65
    Refusal to Submit to Testing 63
    Rehabilitation 64
    Testing Forms 59-62
Annual Inspections 75-77
Annual Review of Driving Record 45
Area of Impact 128
Background Checks (see Driver Qualifications)
Bill of Lading 69
Black Box (see Engine Control Module)
Broker Liability 28
Buses 83, 126
Bus Passengers 126
Cargo Shift 30-31, 77-78, 118
Cellphone Evidence 135-136
Checklists 140-145
    Driver Application 140
    Driver Qualification File 141
    Electronic Data 142
    Record Retention 143
    Trucking Claims 144-145
Commercial Driver's License (CDL) Manual 47-54
    Backing a Tractor-Trailer 47
    Claims Related to Violations 34-36
    Crossing Traffic 50
    Driving in Fog 54
    Driving in Rain 53
    Failure to Maintain Lookout 48
    Following Too Closely 49
    Lane Change 49
    Nighttime Driving 52-53
    Stopping Distance 52
    Stopping on Side of Roadway 51
Complaint, Filing of 119-120
Computer Systems 97-108
    Driver Master 100
    GPS Tracking 102-103
    Load Information 99
    Messages 97-98
    Movement Display 104
    Retention of Data 108
    SensorTrac Data 105
    Tractor Master 101
CSA System 14-19
Daily Inspections 73-75
Dash Cam Video 107
Deposition
    Safety Director 138
    Truck Driver 137
Discovery 120
Dispatch, Unsafe or Forced 73
Disqualification of Drivers 42
    MVR with Disqualifications 28
    Traffic Violations 42
Distractions, Driver 37
    Cellphone Use 37, 81, 135-136
    Texting 37, 81, 135-136
DOT Post-Accident Inspection 72
Driver Fatigue 33-35
    Driver's Logs 67-69
    Duty of Carrier 33-35
    Electronic Logs 34, 68-69
    Exceptions 66-67
    Hours of Service 66-69
    Negligence, Basis of 33-35
    Violations 69
Driver Qualifications 38-46
    Annual Review 45
    Checklists 140-141
    Disqualification 42
    Driver's Application 38
    Driver's License 43
    Driver's Qualification File 46
    Driving History 38-41
    Duty to Notify Carrier 46
    Entry Level Driver 42
    Medical Card 44
    Minimum Standards 41-42
    MVR with Disqualification 26
    Negligence, Basis of 24-27
    Physical Requirements 43-44
    Road Test 40
    Screening, Pre-Employment 38-41
    USIS Report 25
    Work History 38-39
Driver's License, Commercial 43
    Endorsements 43
Driver's Logs (see Driver Fatigue)
Drug Testing (see Alcohol & Controlled Substances)
Electronic Data Checklist 142
Employer Liability 18
End of Day Report 73-74
Electronic Control Module (ECM) 90-96
    Hard Braking Event 93-95
    Last Stop Record 95
Evidence, Preservation of 36-37, 119, 146-148
Experts, Trucking 120
Fatigue (see Driver Fatigue)

Equipment
    Axles 87-88
    Brakes 84-85
    Frames 87-88
    Fuel Systems 87
    Intermodal 83
    Lights 83-84
    Mirrors 87
    Miscellaneous Equipment 89
    Radar Detector 89
    Rear Guards 85-86
    Reflectors 83-84
    Retroreflective Sheeting 83-84
    Speedometer 89
    Steering Systems 87-88
    Tires 88
    Towing Devices 88
    Windows 87
Federal Motor Carrier Safety Regulations (see Safety Regulations)
FOIA Request to FMCSA 149
Forklift Accidents 121-124
Garbage Trucks 124-125
GPS Tracking 102-103
Handling a Trucking Case 119-120
Hazardous Materials 82
Hiring, Negligence (see Negligent Hiring)
Hours of Service (see Driver Fatigue)
Imputed Liability 18-22
Inspections 73-77
    Annual Inspection 76-77
    Daily Inspection Report 74
    Duty to Inspect 29
    Pre-Trip Inspection 73-74
    Negligence, Basis of 29
Insurance 109-114
    Cancellation of Policy 111-112
    Certificate of Insurance 114
    Direct Action Against Insurer 113
    Minimum Limits 109
    MCS-90 Endorsement 109-111
    Negligent Hiring against Insurer 28-29
    Passenger Exclusions 113
Intermodal Equipment Operators 83
Interstate Motor Carriers, Information on
    Agent for Service of Process 15
    Background Information 10-12
    Definition 5
    FOIA Request to FMCSA 149
    Lease, Owner/Operator 22
    Licensing & Insurance 13
    OP-1 Form 6
    Registration 5-6
    Safety Information 8-16
    Safety Management System 14-19
    Safety Ratings 7
Lease Liability 18-22
    Exclusive Control 18-19
    Logo Liability 18-19
    Passengers/Drivers 21
    Scope of Agency 21
    Written Leases, Owner/Operator 20
Left Turn Case 115

Licensing & Insurance 13
Lights Activated on Vehicle 129
Loading of Vehicles 77-78
    Shipper Liability 30-31, 78
Logo Liability 18-19
Maintenance, Negligence (see Negligent Maintenance)
Manufacturers
    Rear Guards 85-86
    Retroreflective Sheeting 83-84
    Towing Devices 88
MCS-90 Endorsement 109-111
Medical Review Officer (MRO) 60-62
Negligent Hiring, Entrustment, or Retention 22-27
    Admission of Agency 26
    Criminal Background Checks 26
    Definitions 22
    Disqualifications of Drivers 26-27, 42
    Driver Qualifications 22, 39-46
    Duty to Investigate 22
    Entry Level Drivers 42
    Insurance Companies, Claim against 27-28
    PSP Report 23
    USIS Report 25
Negligent Inspection, Maintenance or Repair 29
    DOT Post-Accident Inspection 72
Nighttime Accidents
    CDL Manual 52-53
    Re-enactment 131-134
OP-1 Form 6
Out-of-Service Vehicles 72-73
Passengers 81
    Exclusions, Insurance 113
    Unauthorized 81
Perception/Reaction Time 131
Physical Requirements for Drivers 43-44
Pre-Trip Inspections 73-74
PSP Report 23
Preventability Analysis 139
Punitive Damages 37
Radar Detector 89
Railroad Tracks 81
Rear End Collisions 117
Record Retention Checklist 143
Reenactments 131-134
Registration of Carriers 5-6
Repair, Negligence (see Negligent Repair)
Respondent Superior 18
Road Test 40
SAFER System 8-16
Safety Fitness Ratings 7
Safety Record 8-19
Safety Regulations 70-89
    Annual Inspections 75-77
    Cell Phone Use 81
    Daily Inspection Report 73-74
    Dispatch, Unsafe 73
    End of Day Report 73-74
    Equipment (see Equipment)
    Exemptions 70-71
        Non-exempt Commodities 71
    Hazardous Materials 82
    Loading of Vehicles 77-78
    Negligence, Basis of 29-30

      Out-of-Service Vehicles 72-73
      Pre-Trip Inspections 73-75
      Railroad Tracks 81
      State Law 71
      Texting 81
      Warning Devices for Stopped Vehicles 51,
         79-80, 116-117
      Weather Conditions, Adverse 80
SensorTrac Data 105
SMS Results 14-19
Shipper Liability 30-31
Skidmarks 127
Speed Calculations 131
Spoliation 36-37, 146-148
Straight Truck 30
Texting 37, 81, 135-136
Towing Devices 88
Triangles, Caution 51, 79-80, 116-117
Trucking Cases, Types of 115-118
      Cargo Shift 118
      Improper Maneuvers 118
      Left Turns 115
      Rear End Collision 117
      Stopped Trucks 117
      Underrides 115-116
Trucking Claims Checklist 144-145
Underride Cases 115-116
Uniform Carrier Registration System 7-8
USIS Report 25
Vicarious Liability 18
VORAD 106
Warning Devices for Stopped Vehicles 51, 79-80,
      116-117
Weather Conditions, Adverse 80
Work Vehicles 30, 71
      Landscape Trailers 30
      Straight Trucks 30
      Utility Vehicles 30
      Vans 30

NOTES